THE TRINITY
RETRIEVING THE
WESTERN TRADITION

Neil Ormerod

THE TRINITY

RETRIEVING THE WESTERN TRADITION

MARQUETTE
UNIVERSITY
PRESS

Professor Neil Ormerod is Head of the Sub-faculty of Theology and Philosophy,
Mount St. Mary Campus, Australian Catholic University,
Strathfield, Sydney, New South Wales, Australia

Marquette Studies in Theology
No. 48
Andrew Tallon, Series Editor

Library of Congress Cataloging-in-Publication Data

Ormerod, Neil.
    The Trinity : retrieving the Western tradition / Neil Ormerod.
        p. cm. — (Marquette studies in theology ; no. 48)
    Includes bibliographical references (p.   ) and index.
    ISBN-13: 978-0-87462-725-1 (pbk. : alk. paper)
    ISBN-10: 0-87462-725-7 (pbk. : alk. paper)
        1. Trinity—History of doctrines. 2. Theology, Doctrinal.   I. Title.
    II. Series: Marquette studies in theology ; #48.
    BT109.O76 2005
    231'.04409—dc22

                                                                2005025655

Cover photo of the Abbaye de Fontenay (Montbard), France,
by Andrew J. Tallon, 2004.

♾The paper used in this publication meets the minimum requirements of the
American National Standard for Information Sciences—
Permanence of Paper for Printed Library Materials, ANSI Z39.48-1992.

Association of American
University Presses

MARQUETTE UNIVERSITY PRESS
MILWAUKEE

The Association of Jesuit University Presses

Table of Contents

Preface

This work grew out of courses I have taught at the Catholic Institute of Sydney over the past four years. These courses allowed me to appreciate more fully the significant issues in Trinitarian theology, and the ways in which various theologians have responded to those issues. One course in particular, on Trinity in the Western tradition, focussed on the contribution of Augustine, Aquinas and Karl Rahner. Teaching this unit crystallised the present project. I am particularly grateful to the students who struggled with me over the issues in this course. It became clear to me (if not my students) then that the Western tradition still had a major contribution to make to contemporary Trinitarian theology.

This project began life as a series of four research papers, which formed the first drafts of a number of chapters that follow. These are:

"The Psychological Analogy for the Trinity—At Odds with Modernity," *Pacifica* 14 (2001) 281–94 (Chapter 4).

"Augustine and the Trinity—Whose Crisis?" *Pacifica* 16 (2003), 17–32 (Chapter 2).

"Wrestling with Rahner on the Trinity," *Irish Theological Quarterly* 68 (2003), 213–27 (Chapter 6).

"Augustine's *De Trinitate* and Lonergan's realms of meaning," *Theological Studies* December 64 (2003), 773–94 (Chapter 3).

(Reproduced material is used with the permission of the publishers.)

The articles are not just reproduced. They have been reworked, often with some significant additions, to fit the present context, and alterations, in light of further thought and research. I have added an introductory chapter that sets the scene for the later chapters; a chapter on the doctrine of appropriations, which has not appeared elsewhere;

and a conclusion that seeks to identify some future directions. Overall I have attempted to bring the Western tradition into constructive and critical dialogue with contemporary Trinitarian thought. I also hope that some of the material, particularly Chapters 3 and 5, make a positive theological contribution to that tradition.

Apart from my students mentioned above there are others whom I would like to thank for their encouragement and assistance. In particular I would like to thank Professor Tony Kelly of Australian Catholic University who has been my mentor and friend, and Professor Robert Doran of the Lonergan Research Institute in Toronto. Both have been very encouraging in their responses when the initial research articles that formed the basis of this work were being written. I would like to thank Dr Anne Hunt and Paul Oxley for their care in reading and commenting on the manuscript and to Paul also for introducing me to the bibliographical program Endnote. I would also like to thank Jos. Lam Cong Quy OSA of the Augustinus-Institut, Würzburg for his assistance with the work of Johannes Brachtendorf, particularly in relation to Chapter 3. Finally I would like to thank Mr Rohan Curnow for his assistance and care in the transformation of the text from one referencing system to another. However, as always, I take final responsibility for the contents of this work.

There is one aspect of the Western tradition on the Trinity that needs comment but about which I feel powerless to act in the present work. From the Scriptures, through the early Fathers and up until the present generation, the tradition has used the gendered language of Father and Son for the first and second persons of the Trinity. Feminist critique has rightly made us sensitive to the power of language to include and exclude people from our religious discourse and nowhere is this more a difficulty than in our talk about God, and particularly God as triune. All the traditional sources used in this book use gendered language without any sense of self-consciousness and it can be extremely difficult not to follow their example, particularly in identifying the first and second persons of the Trinity. My personal preference is to use the less gendered term Logos, for the second person, and I do so wherever it is possible. However overall we theologians may need to struggle on until poets and mystics can provide a more workable solution.

Let me conclude with an acknowledgement that this is an argumentative book, perhaps even polemic at times. I apologise to those whom I may have offended if at times my words were immoderate or intemperate. It is not my intention to impugn the Christian faith of any of those I criticise. Whatever problems I may identify arise, I believe, not from any unorthodoxy of belief, but in the methodological and speculative problems with which contemporary theology is faced. We are in the midst of massive cultural upheavals and we live in a time when it is near impossible to find our bearings. It remains my conviction that within that turmoil the Western tradition, exemplified in the Trinitarian writings of Augustine and Aquinas, remain a permanent achievement, from which we can continue to learn.

Abbreviations

DS – Denzinger's *Enchiridion Symbolorum*, 33rd ed.

DT – Augustine's *De Trinitate*. Throughout I have used Edmund Hill's translation (Augustine 1991), *The Trinity* (Brooklyn, NY, New City Press), unless I am quoting from a third party. Used with permission of the copyright holder, the Augustinian Heritage Institute.

EN – Pope Paul's VI's Apostolic Exhortation *Evangelii nuntiandi*

FR – Pope John Paul II's Encyclical *Fides et ratio*

LG – Vatican II Dogmatic Constitution on the Church, *Lumen gentium*

ST – Thomas Aquinas' *Summa Theologiae*. Throughout I have used the translation of the English Dominican Province, ©1947 by Benziger Brothers.

Chapter 1:
Trinity—Retrieving the
Western Tradition

Every Sunday Catholics around the world, whatever their differences in nationality, race, social status and gender, stand together to profess a common witness to the apostolic faith of the Church, the Nicene Creed. With one voice they proclaim:

> We believe in one God the Father almighty, creator of
> heaven and earth …

How easy and straightforward it all seems. Yet within the Western theological tradition that lies at the heart of Catholic theology, this apparently simple statement is full of ambiguities and qualifications, of which most believers are completely unaware. Something of this tension is captured through a comparison with the *Credo of the People of God* written by Pope Paul VI, which begins with: "We believe in only one God, Father, Son and Spirit, creator …". The reasons for this change, from naming the Father as creator, to speaking of the one God, Father, Son and Spirit as creator, can be found in a profound shift in thinking in Western theology, born largely in the writings of Augustine of Hippo and continued in the work of Thomas Aquinas. It marks a shift from an earlier stance, one that continues in the Eastern tradition, of beginning with God the Father as the source of all that is.

Up until the 20th century, the writings of Augustine and Aquinas dominated the Western Catholic tradition. Like an impregnable fortress they stood against the shifting sands of theological conflicts, presenting an apparently permanent achievement that withstood the arguments of every opponent. Still, as often happens with intellectual traditions, it began to look as if its time had come, as theologian after theologian turned against it. They have sought alternative sources of inspiration, in particular drawing deep from the wells of the Eastern Orthodox tradition. Influential Catholic theologians such as Karl

Rahner expressed a preference for the Eastern position, claiming it as more biblical than that of the West (1974, 58). Protestant theologians such as Colin Gunton, seeking alternatives to the Catholic tradition, have plundered the Eastern tradition, mediated through the writings of John Zizioulas (1985; 1994). The Cappadocian Fathers, Basil the Great, Gregory of Nyssa and Gregory Nazianzen are now the preferred authors, while Augustine stands condemned for failing to understand their achievements, and so perverting the Western tradition which stands on his shoulders. A variety of sins are laid at the feet of the Western tradition. Its emphasis on divine unity is suspected of modalism. The introspection of psychological analogy anticipated Descartes in promoting modern individualism, a criticism raised by theologians such as Jürgen Moltmann (1981) and Colin Gunton (1997). The *filioque*, the assertion that the Spirit proceeds from the Father and the Son (in Latin, *filioque*), promotes the dominance of institution over charism, of structure over Spirit, and even underpins the structural dominance of the papacy.[1] On every side the Western tradition is assailed. Can it survive and does it still have anything to say to the current generation of theologians?

The purpose of this book is to say that it can survive and that it remains relevant to current theological debate on the Trinity. In propounding this position it is not enough to simply re-state the Western tradition, as if the 20th century had never happened, as if the inherent virtues of Augustine and Aquinas will be so transparent that people will soon see the errors of their ways and return the Western tradition to its former glories. Rather it must be brought into contact with its numerous detractors, to speak and to learn, and find new ways of expressing its profound insights into the triune God. This will involve engagement, dialogue and debate with the many voices finding their place in the current theological environment. Nonetheless it is my conviction that the Western tradition, whatever its weaknesses, remains the most intellectually coherent, indeed compelling, theological account of the Trinity.

The Western Tradition—Key Features

What then are the key features of this Western theological account of the Trinity? How do these differ from the Eastern position and those of current theological discourse? I would like to summarise these key features now, as a point of reference for the later chapters, and to begin to clarify the basic Trinitarian issues that will form the core of the discussion and debate.

The immanent Trinity

A key feature of the Western tradition is its focus on the immanent Trinity (God in Godself), not necessarily to the exclusion of the economic Trinity (God in relation to us), but certainly to its benign neglect. This shift from economic to immanent Trinity is justified by reference to the dogmatic tradition that found it insufficient to remain at the level of the divine economy of salvation. Unless the distinctions we encounter in the economy are real distinctions in God's own being, then God has not really revealed Godself to us. Thus the shift to an account of the immanent Trinity can be viewed as an essential element in the rejection of modalism, according to which God reveals Godself to us in a variety of modes or masks. As faith seeking understanding, the Western tradition has focused on the intelligibility and the plausibility of the notion of an immanent Trinity. If belief in a three-fold distinction within the Godhead is a central element of Christian faith, how can we make sense of such a claim? Is such a claim plausible? Implicit in such a question is the belief that Christian doctrines are not just arbitrary matters of fact, or comprise a complex religious myth, but are shot through with meaning, with intelligibility, indeed so richly meaningful that we cannot hope to grasp their fullness. But such a stance does not deter the search for meaning and intellectual coherence. Rather it pushes the search to the limit, confident that there is an inexhaustible vein of meaning to be found.

On the other hand this focus on the immanent Trinity had the effect of removing theological discourse on the Trinity from our human encounter with God in the economy of salvation. Without this contact, Trinitarian theology appeared remote and irrelevant. Recent theological works have sought to overcome this problem by reconnecting our encounter with the Trinity in the economy of salvation with the immanent Trinity. Most famously, Rahner proclaimed, the "economic" Trinity is the "immanent" Trinity, and vice versa (Rahner 1974, 22).[2] This theological axiom has had its positive and negative consequences, as I shall argue later on. However, it has become the starting point for much contemporary Trinitarian theology as it moves away from the previously prevailing Western tradition.

Nonetheless, the questions raised and addressed by the Western tradition remain and their force cannot be turned aside so quickly. Rahner never intended his axiom to lead to a denial of the reality of the immanent Trinity. Rather it was an affirmation of the fact that distinctions we encounter in the economy of salvation are real distinctions within God. The question of the coherence of belief in an immanent Trinity cannot be brushed aside, without a concomitant brushing aside of the overall intelligibility of faith itself. Put simply, the less concerned we are with the intelligibility of faith, the less concerned we will be with the immanent Trinity. While such a lessening of concern was unthinkable within the era of the Western tradition, it has become almost *de rigueur* in our post-modern age.[3] Further, it may be that the intellectual struggle involved in seeking to understand the immanent Trinity is part of the gain we make through revelation itself. In this way revelation can have a larger cultural impact. With its insistence on the intelligibility of faith, perhaps we still have something to learn from the Western tradition.

The relationship of dogma and theology

One thing that can be said about the Western tradition is that it knew what it believed. To settle matters of belief, you ask the relevant authority such as Scripture, Church creeds and dogmas, papal teaching or the early Church Fathers. An appropriate verse or two of Scripture, or a reference to a dogmatic definition and you knew where you stood. With regard to the Trinity one would know that there is one divine substance (*substantia*) or essence (*essential ousia*) or nature (*natural physis*) and three persons or perhaps *hypostases*.[4] However, there is more to the dogmatic framework than this. Reference to the creed would also produce notions of procession, so that the Son proceeds from the Father, "God from God, Light from Light, true God from true God," and the Spirit proceeds "from the Father and the Son," at least in the Western tradition. This *filioque* addition to the creed began life as a piece of Augustinian theology but was eventually adopted within the creed to become, at least in the West, an element of Catholic dogma.[5]

These elements of belief, three persons, two processions and one God were accepted as dogmatic truths of faith. One task of theology was to "prove" these truths by reference to the sources and defend them against the distortions of the "heretics" who denied these truths.

As well, there was another theological task which consisted in clarifying the meaning of the key terms and their interrelationship. This was a process of logical clarification and exposition, excluding some meanings and promoting others, but basically operating within the framework provided by the dogma itself. At this level the major achievement of the tradition was the introduction of the notion of relations to clarify the distinction of persons. This achievement is found in the work of the Cappadocians, but is presented more coherently and systematically in Augustine and Aquinas. While this task of clarification could not claim to be dogma, its "truth" was as certain as could be hoped for, since it involved basically a logical clarification of the truth of dogma. These two tasks constituted what became known as dogmatic theology.

The theological process, however, remains incomplete if this is all that is done. Theology proper was not concerned just with knowing the truths of faith. Rather, theology is "faith seeking understanding." The Western tradition grasped a clear distinction between the certainty of faith and the more speculative theological task of understanding what faith held to be true. This "seeking" began by noting that a full and comprehensive understanding of the Trinity could never be attained this side of the beatific vision. Still, in this life one could find ways of understanding the mysteries of faith, either through the judicious use of analogies drawn from the created order, or by linking the various divine mysteries to one another, aims of speculative theology given ecclesiastical approbation at Vatican I (DS 3016). Both processes could deliver to the believer a limited but fruitful understanding of what was held as true by faith.[6]

This way of operating has largely broken down in contemporary theology. The emergence of historical consciousness has meant that theologians can no longer appeal in any naïve or direct manner to the Scriptures or the dogmatic formulations of the early Church Councils. Now they can only access the Scriptures through the mediation of the tireless efforts of Scripture scholars who help locate the meaning of the text in its original social and historical context. Church councils now appear as historically limited and culturally conditioned statements that must be reviewed, reinterpreted and even re-evaluated in our modern setting.[7] The work of the Church Fathers is now the province of an army of patristic scholars, who know the Fathers' strengths and weaknesses, their successes and failures, and these scholar's work must be appropriated by the theologian before any positive statement can be made. The appeal to authority, which was so central to the Western tradition, now must face the glare of a hermeneutic of suspicion. Who claims authority? What interests do they represent? Whose interest is served by this definition of faith? (Boff 1978, 265). The dogmatic tradition of the past no longer elicits the automatic assent of theologians.

This breakdown has had a profound impact on our understanding of the theological task. Whereas the Western tradition knew what it believed, contemporary theology feels at times as if it must start from scratch. If the dogmas of the past no longer appear as "facts," perhaps there are other "facts" to be uncovered; or the dogmas provide us with "models," which we then place along side other "models" to provide a new perspective. And so theologians of various persuasions seek to uncover new patterns in the Scriptures which would relativise the *filioque* (such a relativising can be found in the writings of Jürgen Moltmann, David Coffey and Thomas Weinandy, to name a few. Detailed references will be given in Chapter 6). Or the notion of relations is given an interpersonal valence which radically shifts our conception of the Trinity towards a social Trinitarianism. Some adopt a coherence theory of truth which eliminates the distinction between the tasks of determining truth and grasping an understanding of that truth (Pannenberg 1991, 1:21–22). And so the classical understanding of theology as faith seeking understanding becomes a confused and somewhat circular process since coherent understanding itself becomes the criteria of the truth of faith.

Whatever the shortcomings of the Western tradition at least it had a clear conception of the theological project. The differences between this tradition and the current theological environment will become more apparent in subsequent chapters as this tradition is brought into dialogue and debate with modern writings. However, without bringing this difference to the fore, much of the dialogue would be to cross-purposes. As to which approach should be adopted, this raises deeper questions about a theology of tradition that go beyond the scope of the present study. The fact that the approach of the Western tradition stood unquestioned for centuries no longer carries weight but neither does it allow us to dismiss it out of hand.

The psychological analogy

In the carefully delineated distinction between dogmatic and speculative theology, the psychological analogy for the Trinity, first enunciated by Augustine and refined by Aquinas, falls clearly into the latter category. It is a paradigmatic example of faith seeking understanding. Given the dogmatically given data, one God, three persons and two processions, how can we understand this mystery in a way which does not eliminate the mystery but which at least sheds some light upon it? The answer given by Augustine and Aquinas was to find analogies for the Trinity in the operations of the human spirit, for example, the procession of a word from an act of understanding, and the procession of love from goodness affirmed by that word.[8] This highpoint of Augustinian speculation became the central organising principle of Aquinas' Trinitarian work in the *Summa Theologiae*. While it could never prove the fact of the Trinity, nor was it ever meant to, it at least provided a plausibility structure, something that affirmed that our belief in the Trinity is not completely unreasonable. It also proved a useful guide in relating the immanent Trinity to the works of creation and redemption, though often this part of the theological project was neglected.

Now, in the hands of Augustine and Aquinas, the psychological analogy was a major cultural achievement. Embedded within it is a wealth of philosophical stances which challenge every age to raise itself to the height of these great minds. It is not surprising that it was domesticated, distorted and ultimately rejected by those who were not equal to its challenge. Neo-scholastic metaphysics obscured the fact that what ultimately was at stake were certain psychological facts, whose justification lies ultimately in an exploration of human consciousness.[9] In turning their backs on neo-Scholasticism, contemporary Catholic theologians have also largely turned their backs on the psychological analogy. Rahner had no particular interest in it while

Walter Kasper dismisses it in a single phrase, stating Aquinas showed "very great courage" in describing the procession of the Word as an "intellectual emanation" (Kasper 1984, 187). Protestants find it an unwanted intrusion of natural theology into Christian faith, unbiblical, unhelpful and unnecessary. Apart from a few who continue to operate within a broadly Thomistic tradition, such as Bernard Lonergan (1997) and Anthony Kelly (1989, 115–75), it is hard to find a major author who takes the psychological analogy seriously. In the end it is dismissed as merely an illustration, hardly worthy of theology at all (Coffey 1999, 4).

Perhaps nowhere else is the gap between the Western tradition and the modern scene more pronounced. What was so central is now nothing more than an historical dead end, a wrong path taken in the past for which theology must now repent. Many of the sins of the present, particularly modern individualism, are said to find their origins in Augustine's fateful turn to interiority to understand the Trinity. Here the Western tradition struggles most to be heard. Nonetheless there is an intellectual coherence to this aspect of that tradition which, I hope to illustrate, is not matched by many who reject it out of hand. Until that coherence has been matched it deserves our attention, if not our complete assent.

Intellectual asceticism

A wit once commented that the Western tradition on the Trinity could be summarised as follows: "five characteristics, four relations, three persons, two processions, one God and no proof" (O'Collins 1999, 147). Certainly, stripped of the limited intelligibility of the psychological analogy, the Western tradition is remarkable sparse. Reading through the articles of the *Summa* one often gets a sense of déjà vu. Didn't we just deal with this in the previous article? Is this really a different question? The progress is so incremental, the argument so minutely careful that one often seems hardly to have moved at all. Without the psychological analogy it is just bare bones, little more than a structure of interlocking terms and relations. More than this, one might recognise an almost complete lack of appeal to images to sustain the argument. The products of the imagination, expressed in categories of space and time are indeed systematically excluded from the discussion. Where they do appear, they are rapidly deconstructed. For example, Augustine's haunting image of the Spirit as the bond of love between the Father and Son is deconstructed by Aquinas to become another mode of expressing the *filioque* (ST I q37 a2 ad4, q37 a3). Anthony Keaty argues that when Aquinas emphasises the mutual aspect of the love he focuses our attention on the essential love, which is common, and so preserves the *homoousios*. When he emphasises "Father and Son" Aquinas focuses our attention on the notional aspect whereby the Spirit proceeds from Father and Son (*filioque*) (2000). There is a strict intellectual asceticism to this overall project. While the mind cries out for an image from which some insight might emerge, the Western tradition knows that God is pure spirit and as such imagination is a poor guide that quickly leads the mind to error. All that can be trusted is a slow and methodical process of reasoning taking the Scriptures and Church dogmas as their starting point, yet ever on guard lest some stray phantasm of the imagination might deceive us.

Such careful patient reasoning has largely gone by the board. As the mind cries out for images, contemporary theology has not been slow to provide them. Balthasar talks about the infinite space between the Father and the Son, a space for which the Spirit provides a bridge. For both Balthasar and Moltmann, the paschal mystery of the death and resurrection of Jesus is turned into a divine drama of separation and reuniting. For Pannenberg the Spirit is like an infinite field of energy spread throughout space and time, "the supreme field of power that pervades all creation" (Pannenberg 1991, 2:79). Finally much of the present interest in the theme of mutual indwelling (*communio* or *perichoresis*) arises, I would suggest, from the rich imagery it evokes. All these approaches feed our starved imaginations in relation to the divine, but do they bring us any closer to understanding our faith? Or has our imagination taken over the process? Have we confused insight with a satisfying flow of image and affect?[10]

I would propose that perhaps for all its slight conclusions there is something more respectful about the approach of the Western tradition. Often derided for its arrogance in attempting to speak of divinity, the final outcomes are fairly meagre compared with much of what modern theologians assert about God. Perhaps we should be amazed that we can say as much as "five characteristics, four relations etc" and be grateful that we can fill it out with the psychological analogy. It is a small harvest indeed compared to the imaginatively rich theo-dramas of Balthasar and Moltmann. But perhaps it is closer to the mark.

The doctrine of appropriations

At the beginning of this chapter we noted the difference between the opening of the Nicene Creed and the *Credo of the People of God* written by Pope Paul VI. Immediately one notes the difference in attributing creation either to "God the Father almighty" or to the "one God, Father Son and Spirit." At the heart of this difference lies the Western doctrine of appropriations.

The doctrine appears in nascent form in Books 5–6 of Augustine's *De Trinitate*. The presenting problem is a verse from Paul's First Letter to the Corinthians, "Christ [is] the power and wisdom of God" (1 Cor 1:24). Why should this be a cause for concern? Because for Augustine the terms, power and wisdom, are essential terms, that is, they refer to the divine essence. As such they apply equally to the Father, Son and Spirit. So it is not quite right to say that the Son is the power and wisdom of God. Does this mean Scripture is in error? Such a conclusion was unacceptable to Augustine, so his solution is to say that there is a sense in which it is appropriate to speak this way, even though we know it is not the complete truth. Thus we might say that the Spirit is love, or that the Father is creator. These are partial truths, which we retain because of a sense of appropriateness, though we know that Father and Son are equally love and that Son and Spirit are equally creator. As thought in this problem developed, its focus became the doctrine of works *ad extra*, that is, works in the created order, are equally works of Father, Son and Spirit. Therefore, except in certain special cases such as the Incarnation of the Word in human history, we cannot speak of the persons acting in distinct ways in the created order. Nonetheless we might appropriate to them certain tasks or functions as we find in the Scriptures. So we might speak of the Father as Creator, Son as Redeemer and the Spirit as Sanctifier; or the Son as divine Wisdom and the Spirit as divine Love.

As with much of the Western tradition, this approach to dealing with Trinitarian questions is now subject to intense scrutiny. After initial forays by Rahner who sought to overcome limits of the application of the doctrine to works *ad extra*, theologians such as David Coffey, Catherine LaCugna, Denis Edwards and Thomas Torrance have all rejected its constraints in one way or another. The process of appropriation is rejected as arbitrary and unbiblical, otiose and damaging, while a proper theology, which began with the divine economy, would find it of no use whatsoever (precise references to the authors cited can be found in Chapter 5). All this is asserted, despite the fact that Augustine himself began exactly with the divine economy (Books 1–4), and still felt the need to introduce the doctrine of appropriations in some form or other.

Here I think the critics have a point, if a limited one. Certainly stripped of the intelligibility of the psychological analogy the Western approach to appropriation can appear arbitrary and unmotivated; and of course most modern theology has rejected the analogy. However, Christian discourse continues to push Trinitarian language to its limits, and at times it goes beyond the limits of what can truly be affirmed. Nonetheless, this cognitive function of meaning is not the sole function of meaning by which such discourse can be judged. It may be time to reappropriate the doctrine of appropriations within a more modern setting, while remaining faithful to the insights on which it was originally based.

Philosophical not scriptural

The final characteristic for which the Western tradition is often criticised is its preference for philosophical categories over scriptural ones. Indeed even with the debates of Nicea, where the gathered bishops sought to overcome the arguments of Arius, several bishops wanted to reject the term *homoousios* (the same substance) because it was unbiblical (Pelikan 1971, 202). They would have preferred to remain within the confines of biblical language in their rejection of Arianism. It was only when their attempts where found to be futile did they concede the necessity of this "new" philosophical category. For some commentators, such as Alfred von Harnack, this marked the capitulation of the pure spirit of the Gospel to Greek philosophy.[11] Whatever our evaluation of this process it certainly set in train a series of increasingly philosophical incursions into Trinitarian theology. The

Cappadocians introduced the notion of relation, which Augustine then analyses in terms of Aristotle's ten categories (DT 5.2). As I shall note in Chapter 3, the middle two sections of Augustine's *De Trinitate* are dominated by some quite detailed philosophical discussions. By the time we come to Aquinas' *Summa Theologiae* the philosophical mode of discourse begins to completely dominate the account.

Thus in Aquinas the discussion on the Trinity occurs after a thoroughgoing metaphysical analysis of the divine nature (ST I q3–26). For Aquinas, God is perfect being, pure act, being-itself. God is simple, admitting no division or limits. As perfect, God is unchangeable, impassable and eternal, though these attributes are best understood in an apophatic sense, denying any likeness between God and creatures (Burrell, 1979, 12–54). This backdrop of natural knowledge of the divine being colours all subsequent discussion of the Trinity and provides that discussion with a metaphysical rigour rarely evident in contemporary writings.

It is one thing to acknowledge such a trajectory; it is another to spell out exactly how it could have been avoided. Philosophical categories are difficult to exclude all together, as the bishops gathered at Nicea found. Further, a theology that is not explicitly philosophical will tend to import a whole range of philosophical assumptions, many of them very naïve. One is then left with the problem of either making a transition from the language of the Scriptures to that of philosophy, or of producing a mixed discourse which uses now scriptural and now philosophical terms. Hermeneutical difficulties abound in such a process and many attempts to reintroduce "biblical concepts" into Trinitarian theology have suffered in the process. This is particularly a problem given, as we have noted above, the trend in recent theology to relativise dogmatic claims and to conceive of the task of theology as drawing new "facts" about, or models of, the Trinity out of the biblical text.

Certainly one area where this has been most acute is the ongoing theological debate over divine immutability or impassability. This has brought together a number of attacks upon the Western tradition, particularly in light of the Holocaust. Not only is the notion of a suffering God more biblical, or so it is claimed, but only a suffering God can help us make sense of our own history of human suffering.

Protests of this type can be heard from a wide range of sources, from Process theologians, feminist and liberationist authors, to more conservative theologians such as Hans Urs von Balthasar. Speculations of this type move beyond the question of theodicy into the heart of Trinitarian thought, bringing the notion of change and suffering into the Trinitarian relations themselves.[12]

In the face of such difficulties it is instructive to return to the text of Augustine, who manages to keep his different realms of discourse relatively distinct. He knew when he was operating scripturally, when he was thinking philosophically and when he adopted a more interior mode. His different modes of discourse are linked but not confused (see Chapter 3 for details). Aquinas, on the other hand, operates largely within a single philosophical mode of discourse which many moderns find alienating. Both, I think, would have found the recent attempts at a more mixed discourse somewhat confusing and the product of an unclear methodology.

The Modern Reaction

It must be conceded that the Western tradition of Trinitarian theology had fallen into a fairly deep decadence during the late nineteenth and early twentieth centuries. In Protestant theology Schleiermacher had succeeded in marginalizing the Trinity to a mere appendix of his major doctrinal work, *The Christian Faith* (Schleiermacher 1928, 738–51). Among Catholic theologians, neo-Scholasticism reigned supreme. Its a-historical, conceptualist and deductivist approach failed to come to grips with historical consciousness and turned generations of theologians off the dogmatic treatise on the Trinity. The task of revitalising Trinitarian theology fell into the hands of the two giants of twentieth century theology, Karl Barth and Karl Rahner. Whatever criticisms may be made of the work of these two, and there have been quite a number, no one should doubt their achievement in relocating Trinitarian thought back to its central place in theology. In what follows I shall focus, but not exclusively, on the work of Catholic theologians and the trajectories that have emerged out of the thought of Karl Rahner.

The collapse of the immanent Trinity

Rahner is best known for his *grundaxiom*, that the economic Trinity is the immanent Trinity, and vice versa. In its original context Rahner's intent was to challenge the almost exclusive preoccupation of the neo-Scholastics with the immanent Trinity. He sought to establish Trinitarian theology around two foci, the immanent and the economic perspectives. In part Rahner's axiom amounts to the epistemological claim that our knowledge of the immanent Trinity is grounded in the economy of salvation. However, there was also the possibility of a stronger metaphysical claim, that the economic Trinity is metaphysically identical to the immanent Trinity. This highlights the ambiguity of the axiom. On the one hand, the epistemological claim has a strong anti-modalist stance, asserting that the distinctions we encounter in the economy of salvation are real distinctions in God's own being. One the other hand, the metaphysical claim threatens the reality of the immanent Trinity apart from the economy. If there is no economy then there is no immanent Trinity, with more than a suspicion of a modalist account of divinity.[13]

Some would find these concerns realised in the theology of Catherine LaCugna. LaCugna's influential work, *God for Us,* begins by noting that Rahner's axiom "is evoked and endorsed by virtually every theology now writing on the topic of Trinity" (LaCugna 1993, 13). It forms the basis of her own distinction between *oikonomia* (God's relation to us in the economy of salvation) and *theologia* (God in God's own being). For LaCugna the Western emphasis on *theologia* marks the defeat of Trinitarian doctrine, which now needs to be reconstructed with the *oikonomia* as a starting point. From this starting point the traditional language of processions, relations and persons no longer appears necessary to Trinitarian theology, thus casting most of the Western tradition into the shadows. This focus on the divine economy places questions about the intra-divine into the category of inaccessible mystery, a noumenal reality beyond our reach. It did not take long for critics to read a modalist stance into LaCugna's work.[14]

More problematic is the work of Roger Haight. For Haight Rahner's axiom is too strong precisely because it allows us to make an unjustifiable leap from the economic to the immanent. In Haight's work we are left in no doubt that the intra-divine is a completely inaccessible realm and any reference to an immanent Trinity is a leftover from dogmatic and Scholastic theology. Talk of intra-divine processions is dismissed as purely speculative (Haight 1999, 487). Biblical language about the divine Logos and Spirit are reduced to interchangeable symbols of divine presence in the created order, and so tell us nothing about God in God's own being. While Haight claims "not to defend or endorse modalism," this is only because of his adoption of a complete agnosticism concerning God's own being (ibid. 488).

These two authors provide some evidence of the modern trajectory away from concern with the immanent Trinity towards a growing focus on the economic Trinity, precisely as a repudiation of the Western tradition. Of course one could mount a case that what is at stake is a matter of balance and, while some have over-stepped the mark, in general the trend is a healthy one. There are however some deeper questions. To evoke the divine mystery and incomprehensibility runs the long terms risk of making God not 'so full of meaning as to be impossible to grasp completely', but simply meaningless or of turning the doctrine into an elaborate religious myth. This trajectory is certainly evident in the Enlightenment's rejection of historical revelation, its move towards deism and eventual adoption of agnosticism and atheism. What is at stake is whether a real self-communication of the divine is possible or not. Can God really enter into our human history, or is God locked into the divine incomprehensibility to such an extent that God is forever remote from our world? The doctrine of the immanent Trinity allows God to be God-with-us, not through a proxy, but through God's very self. Hence the essential need for a doctrine and a theology of the immanent Trinity.[15]

The relativising of the dogmatic

While Haight criticises Rahner for having too strong a commitment to the Western dogmatic and theological tradition, there are significant ways in which Rahner's writings on the Trinity have relativised that tradition. For all the claims made in the name of "transcendental Thomism," (Rahner 1974, 16 n.12) it is significant that in the whole book, *The Trinity*, Rahner makes only one explicit reference to the text of the *Summa Theologiae* (ibid. 104 n.25). There are several references to Thomistic positions, but generally to repudiate them, for example, his rejection of the psychological analogy, or his criticism of Aquinas' position that any of the persons of the Trinity could have been incarnate (ST III q3 a5). At a more dogmatic level Rahner distinguishes between two starting points, that of the Scriptures and the older (Eastern) creeds, which start with God the Father, and the later Latin tradition which begins with the "*one* God whose *one* essence subsists in three persons" (Rahner 1974, 58). He states his preference for the former over the latter, thus sidelining later, purely Western, dogmatic formulations.

One consequence, as I shall argue more fully in Chapter 6, has been a relativising of the *filioque* among contemporary Catholic theologians. Two important examples of this are David Coffey, whose recent work is the culmination of a life-long scholarly project to reconceptualise the Trinitarian relations (1999), and Thomas Weinandy (1995). What is significant about both these authors is their otherwise patent adherence to a theological style drawn from within the Western tradition. Both engage extensively with the Thomistic tradition, and both are critically dependent upon the work of Rahner, though Weinandy less so than Coffey. Both use Rahner's *grundaxiom* to develop accounts of the immanent Trinity which, to say the least, stretch to the limit the Western dogmatic tradition on the procession of the Word from the Father. Both seek to implicate the Spirit in the Word's procession, largely citing biblical evidence. Whatever the value of this, it is clear there is no dogmatic warrant for it. Coffey goes so far to speak of the dogmatic tradition on the processions of the Son and Spirit as simply one "model" which may be supplanted by a new, more complete model, such as developed in his writings (Coffey 1979, 11–32).

More radical are the suggestions of Leonardo Boff (1988, 204–6) and Gavin D'Costa (2000, 11–23) in regard to the relations between the persons of the Trinity. Both propose a radical symmetrising of the relations between the persons, so that each person can equally be said to have its origins in the others. The basis for this claim is neither the biblical witness nor the dogmatic tradition. Rather it is a rejection of any notion of hierarchy (Boff) or patriarchy (D'Costa) in the Trinity. Now the Western tradition, perhaps even more than the East, is concerned to avoid any hint of subordinationism, but it has never felt the need to completely rewrite its understanding of the processions to do so.

Again what we find here is evidence of a trajectory in modern Trinitarian theology in its movement away from the Western tradition. It is not a case of deepening or reappropriating that tradition in an attempt to communicate its insights to a new world. Rather as key elements of that tradition are denied or relativised the synthesis of the past falls apart, and new, often contradictory positions emerge from the rubble. It is not as if our new authors agree with one another, except in their rejection of positions of the past. Some would welcome this situation as the emergence of a new pluralism from the monolithic positions of the past. Let a thousand flowers bloom! On the other hand the multiplicity of positions speaks of deep methodological problems if there is no way of resolving the contradictions that emerge. In particular questions arise about the status of the Western dogmatic tradition, which did not stop with Nicea and Constantinople. One could also draw attention to those Western Councils which affirmed the *filioque*, for example, the Councils of Toledo (675) and the Fourth Lateran Council (1215).

As well there are the insights of Alasdair MacIntyre concerning the value of operating within an intellectual tradition, as the only way in which substantial intellectual progress can be made (1988). In the terms of MacIntyre, the Western tradition generated by Augustine and Aquinas is a major "tradition of rationality." Similarly Lonergan states, "It is only within the social group that elements accumulate and it is only with century-old traditions that notable development occurs" (1972, 269). It is not just the product of individual intellectual endeavour. Rather it reflects a cumulative collaborative project extending over centuries, dealing with the same questions, the same faith presuppositions. Of course, others contributed to this tradition, directly or indirectly, but it is the work of these two that has best exemplified and prolonged this tradition. To adopt elements of this tradition piecemeal runs the risk of stripping them of their larger context and so distorting their significance. To depart wholesale from it runs an even greater risk of losing the pearl of great price, of starting from scratch to produce an impoverished reflection on Christian faith. These dangers tend to be overlooked in the multiple approaches being developed.

The appeal to the imagination

The work of Hans Urs von Balthasar stands in a dialectic relation to the Western tradition as a whole. Balthasar's theology is *sui generis*, drawing upon an encyclopaedic knowledge of the Church Fathers, the mystics and Western literature and art. He once commented that, while Rahner took the Enlightenment path of the German philosopher Kant, he preferred the Romantic path of the German poet Goethe (Barron 2000, 7). In addition, Balthasar had no time for the dry theology of the neo-Scholastics, a dislike that appears to be reciprocated (Mansini 2000). For Balthasar, faith is not a matter of the assent of the intellect to what is held as true (ST II–II q4 a2), but more a question of grasping the beauty of the form of divine revelation. As a consequence Balthasar is far less concerned with philosophical precision and far more concerned with aesthetic power, which his own theology amply exemplifies. Thus we find in Balthasar's theology a resurgence of the use of categories drawn more from the imagination than from philosophy or metaphysics.

Thus, as we noted above, he speaks of the infinite space between the Father and Son. He views the Trinitarian processions in terms of the categories of "separation and union," while the space between the Father and Son is held open and bridged over by the Spirit. The separation between the Father and the Son becomes the space within which creation and human freedom can emerge. Not satisfied with traditional language of divine immutability, Balthasar views the divine as beyond categories of mutability and immutability, beyond temporality, in a realm of supra-temporality. One area where he concurs in part with Rahner is in relation to Rahner's axiom, which in the hands of Balthasar becomes the opportunity to read into the immanent Trinity every dramatic event of the paschal mystery. This is most evident in his reading of the "descent into hell." What is by most accounts a relatively minor part of the biblical (1 Pt 3:18–20) and creedal (a mention in the Apostle's Creed) tradition becomes a major part of the redemptive work of Jesus, and reflective of an inner-Trinitarian drama.[16]

A similar, though perhaps more radical trajectory can be found in the work of Jürgen Moltmann. Moltmann combines this appeal to the categories of space and time, with the near collapse of an immanent Trinity. For Moltmann the events of the paschal mystery become events which threaten the very existence of the Trinity. In the death of Jesus "the innermost life of the Trinity is at stake" (Moltmann 1981, 81). The economic Trinity not only reveals the immanent Trinity, it has "a retroactive effect" upon it (ibid. 160). We are a long way here from the notion common in the Western tradition of an immutable God, who exists outside the categories of space and time. The immanent Trinity itself is affected by the events of our temporal history.

The appeal to the categories of imagination, to categories of space and time, certainly gives us a theology which is affectively more satisfying. And indeed it can help communicate to us truths of faith about divine love, compassion and forgiveness revealed in the paschal mystery. However the lack of philosophical precision and care may lead us to wonder whether there is anything real about what is being asserted except in some allegorical manner. Is there really "space" in God? Does the immanent Trinity change "retroactively"? To answer these questions requires more than assertion; it requires a careful metaphysical analysis, one which ultimately suppresses any appeal to the categories of space and time. Theology must do more than communicate truths; it must seek to understand them. Without that effort the suspicion will remain that the objects we speak of are unintelligible and ultimately unreal. Christian discourse then becomes just another religious mythology in a post-modern world which is becoming a market place of competing mythologies.

The emergence of social Trinitarianism

Perhaps the most striking trajectory to emerge in contemporary Trinitarian theology is the movement labelled "social Trinitarianism." A key figure is Moltmann, whose work we have already considered above, but others include Colin Gunton (1993; 1997), Miroslav Volf (1998) and John Zizioulas (1985). Much of this work is predicated on a rejection of the Western tradition and a recovery of the Eastern position of the Cappadocian Fathers. The direction of this movement is to replace an "ontology of substance" with the "ontological priority of personhood over substance." Rather than beginning with the divine unity, this movement begins with the distinction of persons. Persons are defined in terms of their mutual relationship and it is through these relationships that the divine unity is constituted. Thus the starting point is not the *homoousios* of the Council of Nicea; rather the divine unity is the result of the *perichoresis* or mutual indwelling of divine persons. For example, according to Zizioulas the Father freely wills his communion with the Son and the Spirit (Fox 2001, 40). Most of the authors in this movement are particularly interested in the ecclesial applications of this revised conception of the Trinity. Western conceptions are said to promote hierarchical and patriarchal Church structures, which suppress the Spirit. The Church should find its model in the egalitarian mutuality of the persons of the Trinity.

Three questions emerge from this movement. The first concerns the historical accuracy of their account of the Cappadocian Fathers. Much of their access to this material has been mediated by the writings of Zizioulas, a noted Orthodox scholar. For example, Sarah Coakley has raised questions as to its accuracy (1999). I cannot claim to be an expert in patristic scholarship, so I shall leave to others the settling of this question.

The second question concerns the validity of using interpersonal categories to describe the inner-Trinitarian relationship. Here again we can trace the possibility of such a use to Rahner's axiom. It is clear that interpersonal categories are valid in speaking of the relationship between the Father and the Son in the economy of salvation. Jesus prays to the Father, is obedient to the will of the Father, and so on. It is possible to develop a rich interpersonal discourse on the basis of the Gospels' portrayal of the relationship between Father and the incarnate Son, Jesus Christ. Is it then valid to evoke Rahner's axiom to draw such language back into the immanent Trinity? Do the interpersonal categories still hold validity in such a shift? Again this is something that requires argument, not just assertion. It is evident that the classical notion of relation used in discussing the immanent Trinity has taken on a significance and meaning never envisaged by those who first introduced it, including the Cappadocians. The classical category of relation now has the connotation of interpersonal relationship. Can it bear the weight?

The third question concerns the validity of drawing ecclesiological conclusions from such an analysis. Here one might have every sympathy with the ecclesiological orientations being proposed by the various authors, though they do not always agree among themselves. Zizioulas, for example, uses his Trinitarian ontology to promote an Eastern Orthodox ecclesiology, while Volf promotes a Free Church model. Nonetheless, one might not feel comfortable with the argument by which they reach their conclusions. Are the Trinitarian relations a good model for ecclesial relationship? Even if we accept the use of interpersonal categories for describing the Trinitarian relationship, it remains an open question whether these relations are a good way to account for church ministerial structures, or the relationship between local and universal church. We are dealing with a different order of reality and the analogies are far from clear.[17]

Again the Western tradition has been far more modest in its approach. Technical terms such as relation have minimal content, little more than pointed arrows (or more technically, relations of origin). As with the appeal to categories of imagination, one must be very careful in how one argues from connotations which are not part of the original notion. Without taking such care it is easy to fall over into tritheism, a charge which is often made with regard to social Trinitarianism.[18] Certainly no one has ever accused the Western tradition of tritheism. It would again raise the concern that modern theologies are developing a refined religious mythology, not constrained by a clear-headed metaphysical analysis.

Conclusion

This book is concerned with retrieving the Western theological tradition on the Trinity, a tradition whose essential elements can be found in the writings of Augustine's *De Trinitate*, and Aquinas' *Summa Theologiae*. It is an essay in aid of such an appropriation rather than a full-blown *magnum opus*. In its own way it will engage with the authors and issues identified above and attempt to bring their work into dialogue with the Western tradition. My own theological guide through most of this project is the work of Bernard Lonergan, himself an outstanding exponent of that tradition and one who has worked creatively to extend and deepen it.[19]

The book will now progress as follows. The second chapter addresses the criticisms made of Augustine by the English theologian Colin Gunton. Gunton's essay, "Augustine, the Trinity and the Theological Crisis of the West" has been inordinately influential in shaping much contemporary opinion on Augustine. I hope to show not only how misguided are many of Gunton's criticisms, but also the superiority of Augustine's theological position to the proposals made by Gunton in that paper. The third chapter proposes a structural analysis of Augustine's *De Trinitate*. This is a more positive attempt to present something of Augustine's achievement, and to understand the challenges his work poses for contemporary theology. The fourth chapter explores the psychological analogy and the very specific challenges it poses to our modern and post-modern world. Here the work of Aquinas will become more prominent in the discussion. This seemingly simple analogy packs quite a punch, and it is not surprising that many have missed its power. A fifth chapter engages with the doctrine of appropriations. This as an attempt to transpose the ancient doctrine in a more modern context by relating it to what Lonergan refers to as "functions of meaning." A sixth chapter tackles head on the work of Rahner in more detail than I have allowed myself above. Again the aim is to argue that overall the Western tradition is more coherent, more comprehensive than the positions of some of its critics. In the final chapter I explore some of the underlying issues at stake in this discussion and the future directions that emerge for Trinitarian theology. Four of these chapters have already appeared in scholarly journals, though they have been modified to fit their new context. I hope I have eliminated unnecessary repetitions of material and arguments, but some repetition will be unavoidable. Each chapter is relatively self-contained on the topic it addresses.

Chapter 2
Augustine and the Trinity:
Whose Crisis?[20]

Augustine has become the whipping boy of much modern Trinitarian theology. It is not uncommon to find all that is wrong with western Trinitarian tradition slated home to his writings on the Trinity, specifically *De Trinitate*. To him we owe our baneful legacy of modern individualism, arising from a modalist understanding of the Trinity, a neglect of the economic Trinity due to an obsessive focus on the immanent Trinity, and so on. We have already identified a number of these concerns in the previous chapter.

An influential article in this regard has been Colin Gunton's "Augustine, the Trinity and the Theological Crisis of the West" first published in the *Scottish Journal of Theology* (1990).[21] Gunton draws attention to criticisms of the Augustinian legacy in the writings of Karl Rahner, and seeks better alternatives in the position of the Cappadocians, mediated through the writings of John Zizioulas (1985). Since the appearance of Gunton's article there seems to have been an effort by Augustinian scholars such as Michel René Barnes and others to rehabilitate Augustine's Trinitarian reputation.[22] The methodology behind these writings has been largely historical. They place Augustine's writings in a proper historical context, pointing out that many of the opinions of the "systematic theologians" are based on outdated scholarship or on otherwise decontextualised readings of Augustine, largely through secondary sources. As Barnes notes, "It is impossible to do contemporary Trinitarian theology and not have a judgment on Augustine; unfortunately this is not the same thing as saying that it is impossible to do contemporary Trinitarian theology and not have read Augustine" (Barnes 1999, 145).

This attempt to set the historical record straight is undoubtedly of value. There have been two significant gains. Firstly, the placing of Augustine within a polemic context, so that his writings can be identified as directed against both Arian and neo-Platonic opponents. Secondly, the inadequacy of the typology developed by Théodore de

Régnon that "western Trinitarian theology begins with (in the sense of 'presumes' and 'is ultimately concerned with') divine unity (i.e. the essence) while eastern Trinitarian theology begins with divine diversity (i.e. the persons)."[23] These historical gains aside, the impression could still be left that at the theological level, the criticisms directed towards Augustine may carry some weight. One could think that the work of the Cappadocians in particular provide a more solid basis for a theology of the Trinity than does the contribution of Augustine who has failed to appreciate the depth of their work.

It is not possible here to deal with all the problems placed at the feet of Augustine's theology of the Trinity. Nor can I match the historical scholarship of Barnes and others who have undertaken a defence of Augustine in this area. However, I do think that Augustine's theology is defensible purely on theological lines. To this end I will undertake two distinct tasks. The first is to engage in a detailed analysis and refutation of key points made by Gunton in his seminal article on Augustine. The second is more constructive and subtle. The common criticism is that Augustine is the father of modern individualism. Much of the source of this lies in his supposedly neo-Platonic method of introspection which is an anticipation of the modern Cartesian turn to individualistic subjectivity. I would like to take this criticism into the heart of Augustine's argument, Book 10 of *De Trinitate*, to argue that far from being "a self-sufficient, or self-constituting subject, the 'alone seeking the alone,'" (Cavadini 1997, 430)[24] Augustine's account of subjectivity is inherently relational.

Gunton and the Theological Crisis of the West

Gunton begins his article with an overview of the problems facing Trinitarian theology in the West. In particular "there has for long been a tendency to treat the doctrine as a problem rather than as encapsulating the heart of the Christian Gospel." Trinitarian theology has been reduced to "a series of mathematical and logical difficulties" where what is needed is more doxological: "glorifying in the being of a God whose reality [is] a communion of persons." The point of his enquiry is "how far responsibility for the state of affairs is to be laid at the door of St Augustine" (Gunton 1990, 34). From these very general comments Gunton identifies a series of problems with Augustine's

theology as found in *De Trinitate*.[25] I would now like to spell these
out and see how they stand up to a critical examination.

Unity over plurality

Gunton begins with the typology of de Régnon, mediated by Karl
Rahner, that "to Augustine it seemed better to begin with the unity
of the divine nature, since it is a truth which is demonstrated by
reason." Gunton finds further confirmation of this analysis in the
translator's introduction to the CUA edition of *De Trinitate* (McK-
enna 1963, vii–xvii). The consequence is that Augustine's theology
always borders on modalism, which he avoids "by the mere assertion
that he does not wish to be a Modalist" (Gunton 1990, 35). While
Gunton acknowledges the "many-sided" nature of Augustine's work,
still there are underlying neo-Platonic presuppositions which head
in this direction.

Let us turn our attention to the text to see if this analysis stands.

Book 1 of *De Trinitate* can reasonably be taken as the "beginning"
of Augustine's theology of the Trinity. Does it begin with an account
of the one God known by reason, as claimed? Indeed, after three
chapters that are basically "scene setting," full of rhetorical flourish,
polemical intent and personal apologia, DT 1.7 takes as its starting
point the Catholic doctrine of the Trinity in basically Nicene and
Constantinopolitan terms: "According to the Scriptures Father, and
the Son, and Holy Spirit in the inseparable equality of one substance
present a divine unity; and therefore there are not three gods, but one
God: although indeed the Father has begotten the Son, and therefore
he who is the Father is not the Son; and the Son is begotten by the
Father, and therefore he who is the Son is not the Father; and the
Holy Spirit is neither the Father nor the Son, but only the Spirit of
the Father and of the Son, himself also coequal to the Father and the
Son, and belonging to the threefold unity" (DT 1.7). As Barnes argues,
the polemic context here is anti-Arian and pro-Nicene (1995). The
majority of Book 1 is given over to a defence of the equality of Father
and Son, through what, by today's standard, is a very literalistic exegesis
of scriptural texts. Most of this exegesis is directed towards a Nicene
reading of favourite Arian texts that implied subordination of the Son,
such as John 14:28. He is concerned with developing a hermeneutical

rule that allows Augustine to distinguish between texts which refer to
the Word incarnate but seem to imply some form of subordination
('in the form of a servant'), and those which refer to the divine nature
of the Word ('in the form of God') (see DT 1.22–31).

It is difficult then to know what Gunton means in saying that
Augustine begins with the unity of the divine nature as known by
natural reason. It may mean that he works out of certain philosophical presuppositions concerning divinity e.g. divine simplicity, eternity,
immutability and so on (see DT 1.3). But these are not his starting
point, which is Scripture and Church teaching. Many of these presuppositions were indeed shared by other Church Fathers and form part
of the intellectual heritage of both East and West. Indeed Weinandy
(1999, 83–112) has detailed considerable evidence from the early
Church Fathers concerning the eternal immutability of God, and of
course the divine unity is asserted by the Scriptures (Deut 6:4).

Materiality a problem

Gunton then turns his attention to what he identifies as "the problem
of materiality." Because of his Platonist predilections Augustine "found
it difficult to believe that the material and sensible realm could either be
truly real or the object or the vehicle of knowledge" (Gunton 1990, 36).
Augustine is more interested in the divinity of Jesus than his humanity,
leading Gunton to a "suspicion of anti-incarnational platonism" (ibid.
37). He identifies a number of aspects of this problem.

Firstly, in dealing with Old Testament theophanies Augustine tends
to minimise any Trinitarian reading of texts, so that, for example, "the
prefiguring of the Son in the Old Testament is not by means of the
Word, but by angels; God is not substantially involved" (ibid. 37).
This mode of angelic action both "distances God from creation and
flattens out the distinctions between the persons of the Trinity" (ibid.
38). Gunton prefers the approaches of Irenaeus and Tertullian in
which "the incarnation and its Old Testament anticipations mutually
reinforce each other" (ibid. 39).

It is difficult to see how this relates to the problem of "anti-incarnational platonism" as Gunton suggests. As Augustine states in Book 1:
"Yet this statement of the faith worries some people, when they hear
that the Father is God and the Son is God and the Holy Spirit is God,

and yet this threesome is not three goods but one God. They wonder how they are to understand this, especially when it is said that the trinity works inseparably in everything that God works, and yet that an utterance of the Father is heard which in not the Son's utterance, and that on the other hand only the Son was born in the flesh and suffered and rose again and ascended; and that only the Holy Spirit came in the form of a dove" (DT 1.8). Augustine does not "shy away" from involving the persons of the Trinity as distinct in materiality, but he is careful to limit this to the New Testament. He is far more cautious than other Church Fathers in reading Trinitarian references into Old Testament texts. Indeed in this regard he is far more modern, strictly limiting revelation of the Trinity to the newness of the events in Jesus Christ. Here Augustine would absolutely agree with Gunton, "some account of the divinity of the historical Christ is a necessary condition of a Christian Trinity" (Gunton 1990, 37).

In fact it is possible to mount an argument that Augustine utilises the reality of the incarnation as an essential element in his anti-neo-Platonic polemic. Such an argument is provided by Basil Studer and Lewis Ayers in post-Gunton articles in *Augustinian Studies*.[26] Further, anyone who has read Book 7 of the *Confessions* will be aware of the central place of the incarnation in Augustine's thought, precisely because it provides a necessary corrective to the pride of the neo-Platonists.

Secondly, Gunton identifies Augustine's handling of the baptism of Jesus as indicative of his inability to treat Jesus' humanity seriously. He states "Augustine cannot handle the story." Here he quotes *De Trinitate*: "It would be utterly absurd for us to believe that he received the Holy Spirit when he was near thirty years old ... but (we should) believe that he came to baptism both entirely sinless and not without the Holy Spirit" (DT 15.46). Again he prefers the position of Basil, who views the baptism of Jesus as a significant event in terms of Jesus' relationship with the Spirit. Augustine, he complains, treats the Spirit "substantially rather than personally and relationally: as if the Spirit was a substantial presence, given in the womb and, so to speak, preprogramming his life" (Gunton 1990, 40).

It is tempting to anticipate an Augustinian response along the following lines: Is it to be suggested that the Spirit was not present at the very conception of Jesus, in contradiction to the Scriptures (Lk 1:34)

(Augustine himself makes this point in DT 2.8)? Should we not say that Jesus "grew in wisdom and grace" as a young boy (Lk 2:52), and that grace is the indwelling of God's gift of the Spirit (Rom 5:5)? And if the Spirit was present at these times, is Jesus not the one whom God gives the Spirit without reserve (John 3:34)? If anything Gunton's suggestion appears adoptionist in comparison with that of Augustine. As to the complaint that Augustine treats the Spirit "substantially rather than personally and relationally," it is hard to know what exactly this implies, and how it could be substantiated or refuted.[27]

The third piece of evidence Gunton presents of this platonic influence is Augustine's use of analogies, which require a withdrawal from materiality. Augustine "judges the material world to be the least adequate source of assistance" in understanding the Trinity. Here at least Gunton is on solid ground. This is the case and easy to document in Augustine's work. However, Augustine is not alone in arguing in this way. Gregory of Nazianzus, one of the Cappadocians Gunton favours, makes exactly the same claim: "The Father is the begetter and the emitter; but this does not mean he undergoes a change, and that there is any temporal succession, or any physical relation. The Son and the Spirit are respectively offspring and emission; for I know of no other terms which could be applied, such as to avoid completely any material suggestions ... 'When did this happen?' Those acts are above and beyond time" *Oration 29.2*.[28] Again we can see Augustine operating out of a common heritage of both Greek and Latin Fathers.[29]

Substance and person

Perhaps no area has become more of a "hot topic" in Trinitarian theology than that of "substance and person." Gunton and others, largely under the influence of the writings of John Zizioulas, will regularly argue for the ontological breakthrough to be found in the writings of the Cappadocians, of the ontological priority of "person over substance." Here Gunton is of no doubt that Augustine either simply did not understand the Cappadocians, or distorted their position because of his neo-Platonic assumptions. "The tragedy is that Augustine's work is so brilliant that it blinded generations of theologians to its damaging weaknesses" (Gunton 1990, 42).

According to Gunton the Cappadocian position implies that the persons or *hypostases* are "beings whose reality can only be understood in terms of their relations to each other, relations by virtue of which they together constitute the being (*ousia*) of the one God. The persons are therefore not relations, but concrete particulars in relation to one another." As a consequence "for God to be is to be in communion" (ibid. 42). Augustine, on his own admission, does not understand the Greek distinction between *ousia* and *hypostasis*, and indeed even has problems with the word "person" (see DT 5.10). Rather than view the Trinity as beings/persons in relationship, Augustine "prepared the way for the later, and fateful, *definition* of the person as a *relation*" (Gunton 1990, 43). To illustrate the "unfortunate implications" of this position, Gunton quotes the following: "The particulars in the same Trinity that are properly predicated of each person are by no means predicated of them as they are in themselves (*ad se ipsa*), but in their relations either to one another or to the creature, and it is therefore manifest that they are predicated relatively, not substantially" (DT 5.12). This position he directly contrasts with that of the Cappadocians, for whom "the three persons are what they are in their relation, and therefore the relations qualify them ontologically, in terms of what they are," whereas the persons in Augustine's approach "lack distinguishable identity" (Gunton 1990, 44–5).

Here Gunton detects Augustine's "tendency towards modalism." Gunton finds that Augustine rejects "what for Basil was the truth about the being of God, that 'three somethings subsist from one matter, which, whatever it is, is unfolded in these three' (VII.11)" (ibid. 45). This leads to the Augustinian position that "the true being of God *underlies* the threeness of the persons" as some form of substratum which remains unknown and unknowable (ibid). It is difficult not to think of Gunton as a little confused here. Surely the position he attributes to Basil, that "three somethings subsist from one matter," does posit a "substratum" of matter which "underlies the threeness of persons."

Complaints such as these are now quite common as a critique of the Western theology of the Trinity, and Augustine in particular, so they deserve a considered response. There are questions about the fairness of Gunton's portrayal of Augustine, but I will attempt to focus on the substantial issues (if the reader will excuse the pun), in an attempt to clarify what is at stake, not just with regard to Augustine, but with respect to much contemporary debate as well. My defence of Augustine is thus theological, not historical or textual, for in the end I hold that his position is theologically more coherent than that presented by Gunton. Moreover, I will draw as much as possible from readily available writings of the Cappadocians to question the criticisms made and conclusions drawn by Gunton.

I am not in a position to question the accuracy or otherwise of Gunton's (or of Zizioulas') characterisation of the Cappadocian position overall, so I will operate simply out of what is stated in Gunton's article. The issue at stake is the problem raised by the terms person and substance in relation to the Trinity. Both terms (in their Latin equivalents) were introduced into Trinitarian terminology by Tertullian, and the terms substance and *ousia* became canonised in the decree of the Council of Nicea which declared that the Father and Son are *homoousios*/consubstantial. Still the meaning of the term remains problematic, largely because of the diverse philosophical presuppositions that are at play. Lonergan has shown how Tertullian's use of the term is influenced by his Stoic materialism, whereas Origen's use reflects neo-Platonic assumptions. For a definitive understanding of the meaning of the *homoousios* Lonergan turns to the rule of Athanasius: "And so, since they are one, and the Godhead itself one, the same things are said of the Son, which are said of the Father, except His being said to be Father" (*Against the Arians*, Discourse III.4). Lonergan regularly expresses this "rule" as "what is true of the Father is true of the Son, except the Father is not the Son." Lonergan notes that for Athanasius the rule was basically a scriptural hermeneutic, so that whatever the Scriptures say as true of the Father is true of the Son and so on (Lonergan 1976, 43–67). However in Basil of Caesarea we find the same rule elevated to an ontological principle. After rejecting any understanding of *ousia* in terms of "pre-existing matter"[30] Basil puts forward the following positive account: "But if community of *ousia* is taken to mean that both are regarded as having an identical principle of being, then it is confessed that light is also the substance of the Only-begotten, and whatever principle of being one ascribes to the Father is attributed also to the Son: if that is taken to be the meaning of community of substance, then we accept the doctrine" (*Contra Eunomius* 1.19).[31] We can see from this exactly why Augustine had problems with the term person, or indeed any term which might be used to identify what is distinct in the Trinity. Put simply, personhood cannot be a "principle of being" because Father and Son (and Spirit) have an identical principle of being. Augustine is well aware of the difficulties, as he shows in his handling of the terms in DT 7.7–9.

How then does Gunton's proposal, that "the three persons are what they are in their relations, and therefore the relations qualify them ontologically, in terms of what they are," stack up against the rule of Athanasius? Gunton's proposal would certainly seem to suggest that personhood is in fact a "principle of being." It seems to imply that what the Father is, is defined in terms of his relations to Son (and Spirit). But if this is the Father's "principle of being" then it is not common to the Son because the Son's relations are different, and the *homoousios* breaks down. Gunton further seeks to clarify his position by speaking of the "distinguishable identity" of the persons. But what is the basis of the distinguishable identity? It clearly cannot be any non-relational property that might belong to the Father, and not belong to the Son (or Spirit). Any such property could then be truly said of the Father, but not of the Son, other than their mutual distinction. Again the *homoousios* breaks down.

It is precisely for this reason that Augustine struggles with the possibility of naming the Father as "unbegotten" in Book 5. At first glance this appears to define a characteristic of the Father that is not true of the Son, but is also not a relational term. Rather it is the denial of a particular relation. It is this realisation which provides Augustine with his solution:

> But because son does not have reference to son but to father, it cannot be what he is called with reference to the Father that makes the Son equal to the Father. It remains that what makes him equal must be what he is called in reference to himself. But whatever he is called with reference to himself he is called substance-wise. So it follows that he is equal substance-wise. Therefore the substance of each of them is the same. And when the Father is called unbegotten, it is not said what he is, but what he is not. And when a relationship

is denied it is not denied substance-wise, because the relationship itself is not affirmed substance-wise. (DT 5.7)

In fairness one can only conclude that Augustine was far more aware of the difficulties to be faced, the nuances needed and the traps awaiting someone doing Trinitarian theology than Gunton and many modern authors are.

Gunton takes up these points later in his article and I shall refer to them now as they further illustrate the gap between Gunton (as well as other modern commentators) and Augustine. Gunton complains that "whereas for Tertullian, Nicaea and Basil the substratum of God is the Father," for Augustine it is the divine substance. Consequently the Son and the Spirit "do not derive their godhead from the Father (they only derive their existence, not their divinity, from him) ... But if the Father is not the substratum of the Godhead, what is?" (Gunton 1990, 57). There are a number of comments one could make concerning these assertions. Firstly, the notion of substratum is not Augustinian; so in that regard the question of what constitutes the "substratum" would not make much sense to Augustine. Gunton refers to the "platonic and aristotelian doctrines of *hypo-* and *hyperkeimenon* [which] presuppose that fundamental reality is other than that by which it is made known" (1990, 57). Again it is difficult to pin down the source of this claim. Aristotle uses the term substance with a variety of connotations. Substance may be taken as *ousia*, which is most intelligible; or then again it may be taken more as substratum, which may point more to materiality and hence is less intelligible. However as Augustine (and the Cappadocians) excludes any reference to materiality (as Gunton himself complains), any Augustinian reference to substance must be taken as what is most intelligible. Secondly, as to whether the Son and Spirit derive their existence but not their godhead from the Father, Augustine would simply not recognise such a distinction in God, for the existence of God is divinity. Finally, as to the question Gunton poses, "But if the Father is not the substratum of the Godhead, what is?," any answer which takes the *homoousios* seriously must answer "divinity." For *what*ever the Father is, so is the Son and Spirit, and *what* they possess in common, *what* they are, is divinity. If however the alternative question was posed, "If not the Father, *who* is?" the answer would undoubtedly be the Father.

For the basic heuristic distinction between substance and person is the distinction between "what" and "who," a point made by Aquinas (ST I q32 a2) and picked up by some modern authors (Ormerod 1993; Helminiak 1986). Modern attempts to build up a "personal ontology" on the basis of Trinitarian doctrine are basically seeking either to reduce the "who" question to a "what" question, or to absorb the "what" into the "who." Either way they will fall foul of the *homoousios*, at least in terms of its understanding as expounded by Athanasius and the Cappadocians. Little wonder that some modern authors now reject the *homoousios* as problematic.[32]

The psychological analogies

It is in the area of the psychological analogy that Augustine would seem to be most vulnerable to the type of criticism that Gunton offers, so it is not surprising to see considerable space given to it in his article. Here the complaint is that the analogies "impose upon the doctrine of the Trinity a conception of the divine threeness which owes more to neoplatonic philosophy than to the triune economy" (Gunton 1990, 45). Thus the "ontological foundations of the doctrine of the Trinity … are to be found in the conception of a threefold mind and not in the economy of salvation" (ibid. 46). The end results of this are "individualism" and "intellectualism." God is conceived primarily as "a kind of eternal mind" (ibid). Gunton repeats his complaints about Augustine's aversion to material analogies, but his main difficulty lies in the following: "In the absence of any other more adequate argument, he makes a final appeal to the triad of memory, understanding and will. The conclusion is inescapable: *The crucial analogy for Augustine is between the inner structure of the human mind and the inner being of God, because it is in the former that the latter is made known, this side of eternity at any rate, more really than in the 'outer' economy of grace*" (Gunton 1990, 48) [emphasis in the original]. Later in the article Gunton will reinforce the point: "All the drive of [Augustine's] thought is away from [the economy] to a knowledge derived from and based in the structures of human mentality" (ibid. 57).

In this we can grasp just how far removed Augustine's conception of the theological project is from that of Gunton. Augustine would never dream of suggesting that the psychological analogies he develops provide a distinct source of knowledge of the Trinity, or that the inner being of God is made known through the structures of the mind. As Augustine repeatedly stresses, our knowledge of the Trinity derives solely from Scripture, mediated through the tradition of the Church (e.g. DT 1.7, 2.2). What he offers by way of analogy is not knowledge but understanding. For Augustine knowledge is derived from the assent of the mind to the contents of the Church's faith. This is a true knowledge but the mind, while it may understand the words that give expression to our faith, does not understand the realities to which they refer. Such understanding is difficult to attain, at best analogous, and is only the product of a long and pious search. It cannot claim the status of knowledge, but remains hypothetical.[33] This same misconception of Augustine's project is evident when Gunton criticises Augustine for a method which begins "with dogma as something given" (Gunton 1990, 41 n.13). It would in fact be inconceivable for him to begin anywhere else, though this does not preclude a long and sturdy defence of the Church's doctrine in the face of Arian counterclaims.

However, not only does Gunton not understand the nature of Augustine's theological project, he also fails to acknowledge the ways in which Augustine's analogies are anticipated in the writings of the Cappadocians. For example, Gregory of Nyssa finds an analogy for the procession of the Word in the word that comes from the human mind: "In a human context we say that a word comes from the mind, being neither completely identical with the mind nor utterly different from it: for it is distinct, as being from it; yet it cannot be conceived as different, since it reveals the mind itself; it is in nature identical with the mind but distinct, as being a separate subject. Similarly the Word of God" (*Oratio Catechetica* 1.2).[34] Certainly Gregory is here seeking an analogy in the operations of the mind, as does Augustine. However, it is not as refined as Augustine's precisely because of its reference to materiality (grounds which Gregory himself would probably acknowledge) when it deals with the procession of the Holy Spirit. For at this point Gregory finds an analogy for the Spirit in the human breath accompanying the production of the word.

As a historical observation, it should be noted that while most of Gunton's criticisms are directed against Augustine's triad of memory, understanding and will, found at the end of Book 10 (DT 10.17), it is not this analogy which proves most significant in the Western tradition. Far more important is the work in Book 9, on the procession of the word and of love from the word. This is terminologically quite different from the analogy of memory, understanding and will, though some of these elements combine in Books 14 and 15. The analogy of Book 9 provides the real template for the work of Aquinas in the *Summa Theologiae*. There are two major reasons for this later movement away from the triad. The first is the misreading of Augustine, found in the *Sentences* of Peter Lombard, which reads the triad as faculties or potencies of the soul. For Augustine however the triad is not meant to refer to potencies but to acts, acts of memory, understanding and will. The second is that the notion of memory retains elements of sensory or empirical consciousness which must be separated out from any divine analogy. Hence Aquinas returns to the analogy in Book 9 as the basis for his systematisation in the *Summa*.[35]

The problem of the *filioque*

Finally we turn to what is a quintessential element of Augustinian theology, the doctrine of the *filioque*. As is to be expected Gunton finds Augustine wanting in his development of this doctrine. Firstly there is the question of its adequacy to the Scriptures, "not in the sense of proving the doctrine one way or another from proof texts" but in giving due justice to "the part played by the Spirit in the economy" (Gunton 1990, 55). More significant however, is Augustine's failure to engage with "ontology." His argument is "an exercise in conceptual mathematics" and "owes more to the structure of memory, understanding and will than to appeal to the economy of salvation." The Cappadocians, on the other hand created "a new conception of the being of God, in which God's being was seen to consist in personal communion" (ibid. 56). Augustine fails to understand this achievement.

As we shall see in the next chapter, Augustine in fact deals with the question of the *filioque* in three distinct ways, one through the Scriptures, one through the logic of relations and finally through appeal to the psychological analogy. Augustine would certainly be surprised to be accused on disloyalty to the Scriptures given he spends the first four books of *De Trinitate* arguing solely from them. As to whether the Cappadocians' position is superior, one might note that none of them provided a consistent and stable solution to the problem of the distinction of the procession of Son and Spirit. On the other hand there are clear precursors to the *filioque* in their writings. For example, in seeking to distinguish the processions of Son and Spirit, Gregory of Nyssa states: "And again we conceive of a further difference from the cause: the one [the Son] is derived immediately from the first cause, another [the Spirit] through that which is thus immediately derived. So the status of the only begotten attaches incontrovertibly to the Son, while the Spirit is unambiguously derived from the Father: the mediation of the Son safeguards his character as Only-begotten, without precluding the Spirit's relationship to the Father by way of nature" (*Quod non sunt tres dei*).[36] There seems to be a clear implication that the Son is involved in the procession of the Spirit in some way, through "mediation." It is also interesting to note that Gunton provides no clear solution to the problem faced by the Cappadocians, and in fact solved by Augustine.

It has become unfashionable in a more ecumenically sensitive age to seek to defend or promote the *filioque*, but it is undoubtedly a distinguishing feature of Augustine's theology and of the Western Trinitarian tradition that builds on his work. In later chapters we shall explore it in more detail in relation to its place within Augustine's theology, in relation to the psychological analogy and its more recent neglect if not demise in contemporary writings. However, at this stage I would like to draw out the *filioque* in terms of the resources developed in the current chapter.

Let us begin with the meaning of the *homoousios* as explained by Athanasius. Athanasius' rule is as follows: "what is true of the Father is true of the Son, except that the Father is not the Son." As we noted above, the initial context of this rule was scriptural, though its sense is generalised by Basil to the following: "whatever principle of being one ascribes to the Father is attributed also to the Son." In explaining the *homoousios* in these terms Athanasius and Basil prescind from any appeal to the imagination in order to ground the notion of substance in truth or being. We must cut off our reasoning from the umbilical cord of the imagination if we are to grasp its full import.

Let us now apply this to the problem of the procession of the Spirit. It is true that the Spirit proceeds from the Father. What is true of the Father is true of the Son, except the Father is not the Son. Therefore it is true that the Spirit proceeds from the Son. Is this a valid argument? Its validity depends on how we conceive of the relationship between the Father and the Son. Does this relationship define the personal identity of both Father and Son? Are there some other relations that need to be recognised in order to specify the identity of either the Father or the Son?

Now at the level of common meaning the terms father and son are mutually correlative. The father is father of the child; the child is the child of the father. No further relationship is needed to clarify their mutual identity. Is this why divine revelation chooses the terms Father and Son to specify the first and second Persons respectively of the Trinity? The Scriptures capture something of this mutual definition of identity when they proclaim, "No one knows the Son except the Father, just as no one knows the Father except the Son, and those to whom the Son chooses to reveal him" (Mt 11:27). We find this same mutuality of relationship in the Johannine Last Supper discourse where we find ample expression of the intimate relationship between Father and Son. Further in the nearly three hundred years leading up to the Council of Nicea, it is clear that the primary question concerned precisely this relationship between Father and Son, which the Council dealt with without the need to introduce any other (extraneous) relationship.

If this is the case then it would appear that the relationship of Father and Son is mutually defining. In this case the argument for the *filioque* outlined above has validity. All that we have used is that the persons are defined in terms of their relationship and the meaning of the *homoousios* as expounded by Athanasius.

However, it might be objected that in fact the argument proves too much. If the Spirit is *homoousios* with the Father and the Son, then "what is true of the Father and Son is true of the Spirit except …" The problem lies in specifying the "except." Here we find that the relationship between Father and Son is different from that of the mutual relationships between Father, Son and Spirit. If the relationship between Father and Son is mutually defining, so that their personal identity is given in the Father being Father of the Son and vice versa, then the Spirit's personal identity cannot be given through its relationship to either the Father or the Son alone. If such a relationship existed it would violate the *homoousios* as expounded by Athanasius, for there would be something true of either Father or Son which is not true of the other, apart from their mutual relationship.

Of course Gunton might dismiss this argument as mere "conceptual mathematics." It is a wonder that conceptual clarity and logic rigour should be dismissed by an appeal to an "engagement with ontology." That the Cappadocians themselves did not finally draw the conclusion of the *filioque* may be more a matter of historical accident than any actual rejection of it. That Augustine did draw this conclusion is a matter of historical fact, and its impact on the subsequent development of Trinitarian thought is well documented.

Book 10 of *De Trinitate* and the Phenomenology of Consciousness

It would not be difficult to continue this catalogue of problems associated with Gunton's criticism of Augustine, but it is far more interesting to take up the challenge posed by Augustine's own writing, in particular at the point where he may appear most vulnerable, in Book 10 where he undertakes an analysis of the mind's knowledge of itself. Here surely Augustine falls into the trap of individualism, the self-sufficient, or self-constituting subject, the "alone seeking the alone." It is also interesting how few of those who have written recently on Augustine have ventured into this dense material.[37] I would like to argue however that in this book Augustine is presenting a very precise phenomenology of human consciousness, and the account that emerges is one of consciousness as inherently relational.

The problem that Book 10 seeks to address is raised at the conclusion of Book 9. Augustine has developed an analogy for the Trinity on the basis of the self-knowledge and self-love of the mind. In keeping with the *filioque* Augustine wishes to have the self-love flow from the self-knowledge. However, in Book 9 he identifies a difficulty, that is, a desire that precedes knowledge: "This appetite, that is inquisitiveness, does not indeed appear to be the love with which what is known is loved (this is still busy getting known), yet it is something of the same kind. It can already be called will (*voluntas*) because everyone who inquires wants (*vult*) to find out, and if what is being inquired about belongs to knowledge, then everyone who inquires wants to know … So parturition by the mind is preceded by a kind of appetite which prompts us to inquire and find out what we want to know, and as a result knowledge is conceived and brought forth as offspring" (DT 9.18). The first few sections of Book 10 (DT 10.1–4) are then taken up with an analysis of this phenomenon, whereby Augustine seeks to prove that in every case this preceding desire is itself a love based on knowledge. However, he still notes that, "These are the reasons why people who want to know something they do not know seem to love the unknown; and because of their keen appetite for inquiry they cannot be said to be without love. But if you look at the matter carefully I think I have truly made out the case for saying that in fact it is otherwise, and nothing at all is loved if it is unknown. However, the examples I have given are of people wanting to know something which they are not themselves; so we must see if some new issue does not arise when the mind desires to know itself" (DT 10.4). Thus our attention is turned to the question of the mind and its self-knowledge and self-love, to see if "some new issue" might appear. At this stage Augustine presents us with his phenomenology of consciousness, or what he refers to as mind (*mens*). The problem is one of how the mind knows itself, given its constant "self-presence," that is, "nothing could be more present to it than itself" (DT 10.5). In modern terms Augustine is raising the question of "introspection."

Immediately, Augustine dispels any similarity with ocular experience. The eye cannot see itself, except it looks in a mirror: "and it is not to be supposed that in the contemplation of non-bodily things a similar device can be produced, so that the mind can know itself as in a mirror" (DT 10.5). Rather the mind knows itself in "the very act of knowing." "It knows what knowing is; and while it loves this that it knows it also longs to know itself. But where in this case does it know its knowing, if it does not know itself?" (DT 10.5): "How comes it then that a mind which does not know itself knows itself knowing something else? It is not that it knows another mind knowing, but itself knowing. Therefore it knows itself. And then when it seeks to know itself, it already knows itself seeking. So it already knows itself. It follows then that it simply cannot not know itself, since by the very fact of knowing itself not knowing, it knows itself. If it did not know itself not knowing, it would not seek to know itself. For it knows itself seeking and not knowing, while it seeks to know itself" (DT 10.5). Augustine is appealing to the mind's self-knowledge, or self-presence in the mind's normal operations, in seeking, in knowing. In these very experiences the mind experiences itself as seeking or knowing. Still the object of this seeking and knowing can be anything. Augustine makes this clear when he returns to the problem of introspection later in Book 10: "And this is its impurity, that while it attempts to think of itself alone, it supposes itself to be that without which it is unable to think of itself. And so when it is bidden to know itself, it should not start looking for itself as though it had drawn off from itself, but should draw off what it has added to itself … Let the mind then recognise itself and not go looking for itself as if it were absent, but rather turn to itself the interest of its will [*intentionem voluntatis*]" (DT 10.11). The key here is the clause, "it should not start looking for itself as though it had drawn off from itself, but should draw off what it has added to itself." Introspection is not a matter of withdrawal from the world. Nor should we seek the mind as if it were not present. Rather it is present in every cognitional act. What needs to be withdrawn, or subtracted is "what it has added to itself," that is, the content of the cognitional act, which varies depending on the object which we are seeking to know. So we seek the mind, not as something absent; rather we require "*intentionem voluntatis*" or willing attention that can identify the presence of mind in each and every cognitional act.

From this we can see that for Augustine the mind is inherently relational. The process of introspection is not withdrawal from the world. Rather, the mind is discovered precisely in its relationships with the objects of the world. Nor does Augustine provide any comfort for those who might think that "the world" means the external world. Augustine's world is constituted by two types of objects, both equally real and knowable, "one the sort that the consciousness perceives through bodily sensations, the other the sort it perceives through itself" (DT 15.21). See also *Confessions* Book 7 where Augustine discovers the reality of the inner world, through his identification of the real with truth, *verum*. There is no inward look, no self-sufficient, self-enclosed subjectivity, no self-absorption. Our self-knowledge is the fruit, not of withdrawal from the world, but of a special act of attention that allows us to distinguish between the object which "it has added to" the mind, and the more primitive self-presence of the mind to itself.

This account of self-presence is remarkably nuanced, and I would add, in my experience accurate. The clarity with which Augustine deals with the problem of consciousness is matched only by that of Bernard Lonergan. In Chapter 11 of *Insight* Lonergan speaks of consciousness in almost identical terms. He states that "consciousness is not to be thought of as some sort of inward look"; his concern is with whether a person "performs certain kinds of acts" not with "the rather remarkable power of looking into themselves and intuiting things quite clearly and distinctly." For Lonergan consciousness is "an awareness immanent in cognitional acts." Consciousness "can be heightened by shifting attention from the content to the act" but it is not constituted by such a shift (Lonergan 1992, 344–45).[38] The parallels here are quite strong.

This is not to say that there are not difficulties with Augustine's account of self-knowledge. They arise because of Augustine's identification of the self-presence of the mind as a form of knowledge, leading him to some difficult problems: "what are we to say then? That the mind knows itself in part and does not know itself in part?" (DT 10.6).[39] Here Lonergan provides a solution by insisting that consciousness, the mind's self-presence, is only a component of knowing, an empirical component, which must be subject to intelligent questioning and reasonable judgment.

Conclusion

Perhaps there are some lessons that we can learn from this analysis of Gunton's article. The first is that many of the criticisms of the Western tradition made by contemporary theologians cannot be taken at face value. Theologians may not have absorbed the latest results of historical scholarship, and they can misunderstand and at times misrepresent the works of that tradition by reading them out of their historical context. Further, there are philosophical subtleties, particularly in DT Book 10, which will go over the head of the unprepared reader.

Augustine's *De Trinitate* is by any estimate a classic. As such, we do not simply measure it; it measures us. If there is a theological crisis in the West at present it may be found it our failure to appreciate such a classic text.

The second lesson is to note how little sympathy contemporary theology has for the theological worldview of the Western tradition. This is evident in Gunton's complaint that Augustine begins "with dogma as something given" (Gunton 1990, 41 n.13). Such a complaint is indicative of the gap that now exists between contemporary theology and the Western tradition. What is surprising is that Gunton appears so unaware of the gap he is unable to enter sympathetically into the theological worldview of Augustine. While we might have difficulties with this worldview because of the modern emergence of historical consciousness, it is anachronistic to complain that Augustine does not share our difficulties. Much contemporary theology reflects this same problem.

A third lesson concerns the place of the psychological analogy. Gunton's grasp of its details and the history of its development appear minimal. Again this is not uncommon among many contemporary theologians. It is too easy and too common to dismiss as a mistake, or historical dead end, what one has not understood. We shall examine the place of the analogies in Augustine's work in the next chapter and its overall significance in the modern context in the subsequent chapter. However the antipathy to the analogy based on the assertion that it leads to a monadic individualistic conception of the person is simply not substantiated by the Augustinian text. Consciousness is always relational for Augustine. Apart from that, Gunton, like most modern authors, is fairly vague about the details of the analogy.

Finally, much is made in contemporary theology of an appeal to the Cappadocian Fathers as a counter to the Augustinian position. It is clear from the above analysis that not all the claims made by appealing to these sources can be supported. The references to the Cappadocians made in the material above would seem to be far more supportive of Augustine than of Gunton. The Cappadocians stressed the need for analogies based on spiritual realities and rejected any appeal to material analogies, which they judged inadequate to the situation at hand. Their understanding of the *homoousios*, in line with that of Athanasius, leads to the same problems that Augustine identified with the term "person" to identify what is distinct in the Trinity. Indeed, it would not be too difficult to make a case that the insights that are scattered in the writings of these great Greek Fathers find a natural home in the more systematic exposition of Augustine.

In the next chapter we shall move to a more constructive task, that of uncovering the structure of *De Trinitate*. In doing so I hope again to highlight not only the genius of the author of this classic text, but also the continuing lessons we have to learn from him.

Chapter 3
Augustine's *De Trinitate* and Lonergan's Realms of Meaning[40]

By all accounts, Augustine's *De Trinitate* is a complex, difficult book. Augustine himself thought that it would only be "understood by a few" (Merriell 1990, 15 n.6). It is clear from the previous chapter that a number of contemporary Trinitarian theologians, for whom Augustine has become something of a whipping boy, are not among the few who have understood his work. Variously misrepresented and frequently misunderstood, a variety of theological sins have been laid at his feet, notably the sins of individualism, with more than a suspicion of modalism. As we have already noted contemporary Trinitarian thought has turned wholesale from the Western tradition championed by Augustine and Aquinas to embrace the supposedly superior position of the East, particularly that of the Cappadocians.

On the other hand, Augustine's *De Trinitate* is no easy text to comprehend. Its fifteen books, which in English translation come to around 350 pages of densely argued theological text, make exceptional demands on the tenacity of any reader. It has also become apparent that the work operates with multiple agendas. While Peter Brown classified the work as speculative—he says it displays "remarkable evidence of Augustine's capacity for speculation" (1967, 277)—more recent scholarship has increasingly noted the polemic context of the work, directed against Arian and neo-Platonic opponents. This same scholarship has also noted the inadequacy of the typology developed by de Régnon that "western Trinitarian theology begins with (in the sense of 'presumes' and 'is ultimately concerned with') divine unity (i.e. the essence) while eastern Trinitarian theology begins with divine diversity (i.e. the persons)" (Barnes 1999, 152). As was noted in the previous chapter, there is far more continuity between Augustine and the concerns of the Cappadocians than many moderns acknowledge. A thoroughgoing, historically sensitive and theologically insightful commentary on the whole of *De Trinitate* is not yet available. Merriell makes this observation while acknowledging the contribution of various scholars (1990, 13–14 n.1). Since Merriell's observation, the work of Brachtendorf (2000) has appeared. This comes close to fitting the bill, but does not pay enough attention to Books 1–4.

One issue which has received attention is that of the structure of the work. This is the question I would like to address in the present chapter. I begin with a review of various proposals that have been suggested concerning that structure. I shall then put forward a hypothesis that suggests a "natural structure," one which relates to the realms of meaning identified by Lonergan in *Method in Theology* (81–85). Indeed the correspondence is so close that one could almost suppose Lonergan had *De Trinitate* in mind when he wrote about the realms of meaning in *Method*. In the process of putting forward this hypothesis I also comment on various features of Augustine's work which are further illuminated by Lonergan's writings.

Proposals Regarding the Structure of *De Trinitate*

It is commonly held that Augustine conceived of *De Trinitate* as a unity. Commentators note that he was annoyed at the early and unauthorised publication of the first eleven and a bit books of the work, because "he conceived it as a whole, as a very tightly argued and structured unity, not at all suitable for serial publication" (Hill 1985, 77).[41] Certainly there are often clear transition points at the end of one, and beginning of each new, chapter. Book 15 gives a summary of the whole, which indicates some sense of plan for the work. Augustine himself describes his method as an *inquisitio*, a search not unlike that later proposed by Anselm, of faith seeking understanding. Augustine was concerned "lest the reader mistake a stage in the search for its conclusion," and hence wanted to publish the work as a whole (Merriell 1990, 16). On the other hand, any personal conception of the work as a whole had to survive the length of time Augustine spent working on the text, a period which is estimated to be over twenty years. Further, modern attempts to uncover the unity of the work, or at least analyse its structure, have produced a variety of responses.

The most common division made in relation to the structure of *De Trinitate* is to distinguish between Books 1–7 and Books 8–15. An older style theology identified the first seven books as concerned with Trinitarian faith and doctrine, and the last eight as involving the use of reason. While couched in the language of neo-scholasticism, this distinction does have some validity inasmuch as there is a turning point reached at the end of Book 7 where Augustine concludes the Book with one of his favourite scriptural quotes, one which characterises the following chapters of his work in *De Trinitate*, "Unless you believe, you will not understand." He then begins Book 8 with an earnest prayer that God "open our understandings." A more useful distinction to make in light of this might be to say there is a transition from Book 7 to Book 8 from what Lonergan identifies as the functional specialty of doctrines to the specialty of systematics (1972, passim). Augustine is not unreasoning in the first seven books, nor is he removed from faith in the last eight books, as I shall argue later. But there is a shift towards understanding what we believe that does occur at this juncture.

Less successful in this regard is the distinction made between the first four books, which are "scriptural" and the rest which draw on human reason. The same objection as above remains for this distinction. Augustine would not recognise this as descriptive of his project, as he seeks the most profound integration of faith and reason, not its sharp disjunction. On the other hand this attempted structural distinction does alert us to the fact that something different is happening in Books 1–4 than is happening in Books 5–7. Any structural analysis must account for this difference.

These two "traditional" structural accounts of *De Trinitate* have been superseded by more recent historically sensitive accounts by scholars such as Edmund Hill, John Cavadini and Johannes Brachtendorf. Hill has proposed a chiastic structure for De Trinitate. In his book, *The Mystery of the Trinity*, he suggests a structure along the following lines (81) (The second column refers to the number of books in each division):

a	1	Book 1: the absolute equality of the divine persons, proved from scripture;
b	3	2-4: the missions of the divine persons, examined in scripture,
c	3	5-7: rational defence of faith so far established, language of relationship etc.;
d	1	8: centre book; attempt to 'storm' God, break surface, emerge from mirror world;
c'	3	9-11: construction of mental image of God by rational introspection;
b'	3	12-14: history of this image in Everyman, and from Adam to Christ, explored in the light of Scripture;
a'	1	15: the absolute inadequacy or inequality of the trinitarian image to the divine exemplar Trinity.

In his translation of *De Trinitate*, Hill spells out the same divisions as a descent-ascent model, a parabola which moves from the scriptural Book 1 through the missions (Books 2–4) to a linguistic and logical analysis (Books 5–7) through the transition in Book 8 to an "inward mode," back to the psychological (Books 9–11) which links with the rational reflections in Books 5–7; to the human image (Books 12–14) linked to the missions as the story of the fall and redemption, and concluding with the scriptural Book 15 (ibid. 27). As is often the case with such chiastic analyses, Hill himself concedes that "it is a little too neat … To speak plainly the six books [Books 8–14] we are here concerned with do not have the clear-cut structure of the six in the first half of the book [Books 2–7]" (ibid. 258). It does, however, have the advantage of being more closely tied to the detail of the contents of the work than the simplistic faith-reason division previously used.

In his article, "The structure and intention of Augustine's *De Trinitate*," Cavadini proposes a more contextual reading of the work. He reads it as a polemic work directed against neo-Platonic methods of ascent to the divine (Cavadini 1992, 103–23). The influence of neo-Platonism on Augustine is evident by his own account in the *Confessions*. Yet that same work displays his dissatisfaction with their approach to God, its lack of humility and its failure to learn from the

Incarnation. Cavadini reads *De Trinitate* in the same manner. While some have found in *De Trinitate* "one of the finest examples of what could be called Neoplatonic anagogy that remains from the ancient world" (ibid. 105), Cavadini draws a more negative relationship: "*De Trinitate* uses the Neoplatonic soteriology of ascent only to impress it into the service of a thoroughgoing critique of its claim to raise the inductee to the contemplation of God, a critique which, more generally, becomes a declaration of the futility of any attempt to come to any saving knowledge of God apart from Christ" (ibid. 106). For Cavadini the structure of *De Trinitate* is built upon this deliberate failure.

Cavadini is correct in identifying a polemic against neo-Platonism operating in *De Trinitate*. That this is part of the overall intention of the author is made clear in the first book, where he speaks of those who "raise their regard to the unchanging substance which is God. But so top-heavy are they with the load of their own mortality, that what they do not know they wish to give the impression of knowing, and what they wish to know they cannot" (Book 1.1). Put simply they are presumptuous. However, Cavadini's approach sheds little light on the first seven books, except as a prelude to the failed attempt at ascent.

In a more recent article, Cavadini shifts his focus from neo-Platonic ascent and its failures to the broader pedagogical themes in *De Trinitate* (1997). He describes the work as "undogmatic, open-ended and experimental" (ibid. 432). He draws our attention in particular to the theme of human beings being made in the image of God, and the movement from inner word to outer word, from the mind's pre-linguistic self-expression to its actualisation "in the world of sign and signification, that is, of culture" (ibid. 434). What is vital for Cavadini is this movement from inner word to outer sign. The inner word is "conceived either in covetousness or charity." If conceived in covetousness or dominated by pride, then it will "inevitably produce cultures which instantiate or express this preference of power over justice" (ibid. 437). The social transmission of knowledge is never untouched by the original intention within which the inner word is formed.

This suggestion of Cavadini, while providing significant insights into a theme present in the work, again cannot claim to represent an account of the work as a whole. He makes numerous references to the text of *De Trinitate*, but the overwhelming majority of them are to the second half of the work. Again the first half is reduced to a prelude to the real issues raised in the second half.

Most recently Brachtendorf (2000) has provided a book-length study of the structure of *De Trinitate*.[42] He places Augustine's work in a neo-Platonic context, in particular the Plotinian doctrine of the mind. This allows Augustine to overcome the emanationist and subordinationist tendencies in neo-Platonic metaphysics through an account of the mind, its self-presence and activities. He begins his account of *De Trinitate* with a commentary on Books 5–7, which Brachtendorf views as an exposition of traditional doctrine in Aristotelian philosophical categories. However, his main interest is in Books 8–15, to which he devotes more than two thirds of his commentary. Brachtendorf argues that Book 9–14 "do not represent an attempt at an ascent to God, but only an ascent to an insight into the human mind in order to reveal how it images the triune God" (Teske 2002, 415). Central to this argument is Book 10 where Augustine overcomes the Plotinian view of human consciousness as self-absorption with a detailed analysis of the mind's self-presence as a permanent, unchanging and constitutive reflexivity (Brachtendorf 2000, 43–44). It is in the structure of this self-presence, consisting of *memoria sui, intelligentia sui* and *voluntas sui*, that we find the Trinitarian *imago Dei*. The distinction between the mind's self-presence and its explicit self-knowledge forms the basis of Augustine's analysis of our human efforts to approach God (Books 11–14).

While Brachtendorf has presented a meticulous and scholarly study of *De Trinitate* there remain unanswered questions. Again, not much attention is given to the early Books, in particular the first four scriptural Books which receive minimal attention. Their place in the overall unity of Augustine's thought is not clarified. Further, while his highlighting of Book 10 and its disengagement with Plotinian accounts of consciousness is a major achievement,[43] I shall argue below there is a shift in Book 12 that requires explanation, to which he does not attend. Brachtendorf gives only eighteen pages of commentary to Books 11–13, whereas a number of other Books receive separate treatment.

Finally, I refer to the work of Donald Juvenal Merriell. In his book, *To the Image of the Trinity: A Study in the Development of Aquinas'*

Teaching, Merriell provides an insightful early chapter on Augustine's *De Trinitate* (1990, 13–35). Merriell rejects the earlier faith-reason division as sundering the unity of the work. He draws our attention to two questions which Augustine raises in Book 1. "First, how are we to understand that Father, Son and Holy Spirit work indivisibly as one God, yet play distinct roles within the created world? Secondly, how can we understand the distinction of the Holy Spirit within the Trinity since we cannot say that the Father or the Son or both have begotten Him?" (ibid. 18). He further notes how these two questions resurface at different places within *De Trinitate*, giving "a specific direction to Augustine's investigation of the mystery of the Trinity" (ibid. 19). These two questions then provide Merriell with a thematic key to unlock the structure of *De Trinitate*. Thus in Book 1–4 he claims the first question dominates, though by the end of Book 4 Augustine raises the issue of the *filioque*, leading to a more extended treatment of the problem of the Holy Spirit, culminating in the designation of the Holy Spirit as Love in Book 6. This insight then dominates the remainder of the work. "The entire search unfolds from the analogy of love in book 8 and is explicitly aimed at the solution of the problem concerning the distinction of the Holy Spirit from the Son by means of the notion of love" (ibid. 25). This approach leads Merriell to stress the unity of the work through the unifying force of these two questions. Still there is an acknowledgement of some transitions with relatively unified treatments in Books 1–4, 5–7, and 8–15.

While I endorse Merriell's suggestion that various themes and questions recur within *De Trinitate*, and that this repetition is an essential feature of the structure of the work, I do not think he has paid sufficient attention to the nature of the transitions and the modes of thought that Augustine is operating out of in the various sections. I suggest that there are four sections to *De Trinitate*, Books 1–4, 5–7, 8–11, and 12–15. Each of these sections presents us with Augustine operating in a different realm of meaning, a category drawn from the writings of Bernard Lonergan. The reason why themes and questions are repeated is that Augustine tends to consider them from the perspective of these different realms of meaning. I hope to illustrate this point with an indication of Augustine's treatment of the *filioque*, which is central to the problem of the distinction between the Son and the Holy Spirit. However, before I put forward this proposal, I must give a brief account of what is meant by "realms of meaning" as conceived by Lonergan.

Realms of Meaning[44]

In *Method in Theology* Lonergan identifies four distinct realms or worlds of meaning, which arise from different modes of conscious and intentional operation. He begins by distinguishing between the realm of common sense and the realm of theory. The realm of common sense is the realm of persons and things in relation to us, peopled by relatives, friends, acquaintances, fellow citizens and the rest of humanity. Its terms are those of everyday language and its operation that of the self-correcting spiral of learning heading towards an understanding of things in relation to us. As common, it is common to a people and hence particular to that people who share a common set of meanings and values. It varies from time to time and place to place. It speaks an everyday language which knows not the intrinsic meaning of things, but the proper use of words in a proper context.

Still, intelligence can demand more. It asks not just how things are in relation to us, but how things are in relation to one another; not just how to correctly use words, but their precise meaning; not just their meaning for this people in this place and time, but their meaning for all people everywhere. And so Socrates asked for the meaning of justice, not just in Athens but everywhere. Under the influence of this systematic exigence, we develop technical meanings and language, which, though they relate to the same objects, do so in a new way. We no longer speak of feeling hot; we specify a temperature. We no longer speak of going faster; we determine a precise acceleration. And so a new realm of meaning develops, the realm of theory. Different communities develop different theoretical realms—scientific, technical, theological and so on. But each is driven by the same systematic exigence, the drive to understand things in relation to other things, not just to ourselves.

The two realms exist in some tension. Lonergan often refers to Eddington's two tables, the solid, coloured table of commonsense, and the table composed mostly of empty space of the physicist. Who is right? Is common sense simply a form of ignorance to be replaced by science, or is science simply of pragmatic value, allowing us to control things without really penetrating to their reality? These questions Lonergan refers to as arising from a critical exigence, and their answers can be found not in the development of a new theory, which would simply heighten the tension, but by moving to a new realm of meaning, that of interiority. This realm is uncovered through an act of introspection or self-appropriation, not as withdrawal from the world, but as a heightening of consciousness, an act of attending to the conscious subject as it engages in its intentional activities. There one can uncover the structures, norms and potentialities of human subjectivity.[45] Mastery of this interior realm can provide one with the resources needed to address critical epistemological and metaphysical questions, and heal the tensions between the realms of common sense and theory. Lonergan notes that the outcome of this self-appropriation resembles theory, but that "as this heightened consciousness constitutes the evidence for one's account of knowledge, such an account by the proximity of the evidence differs from all other [theoretical] expressions" (1972, 83).

Finally Lonergan identifies a transcendent realm corresponding to the human desire for complete intelligibility, unconditioned judgment and a good beyond all criticism. This draws us to a realm beyond those of common sense, of theory and of interiority into a realm of fulfilment, peace and joy in which God is known and loved. This is a realm of religious experience and its expression, culminating in mystical prayer and ultimately union with God.

Application to *De Trinitate*
The Realm of Common Sense—Books 1–4

It is commonly agreed that Books 1–4 are the scriptural basis for Augustine's teaching on the Trinity. It is not unreasonable, I suggest, to read these Books as an exploration of Christian belief in the Trinity within the realm of a scripturally informed, and hence Christian, common sense. Now it is one thing to suggest that Books 1–4 operate in the realm of a scripturally informed common sense. It is another to provide evidence. The first thing to note is that such a designation is not meant to denigrate what Augustine achieves in these books. Augustine's exegesis is incredibly detailed, drawing on his vast storehouse of scriptural knowledge. He draws freely and regularly from the whole range of Scripture to advance the agenda he established in the initial sections of Book 1. Prominent among these are his anti-Arian arguments and his desire to move his readers beyond materialistic conceptions of the divine. It is worth pointing out in this context that Lonergan refers to the work of modern biblical and historical scholarship as a specialised form of common sense (Lonergan 1972, 233). More positively I note the lack of any deployment of technical terms, used in a technical manner. He uses terms such as substance, essence and person, but his deployment of them remains unexamined. They are "common notions," not technical terms. Next we draw attention to Augustine's own understanding of the place of the Scriptures in his argument. He speaks of Scripture as "adapting itself to babes" (DT 1.2) so that it might lead us to higher realities. The Scriptures "are in the habit of making something like children's toys out of things that occur in creation" (DT 1.2) in order to capture our "sickly gaze." Further it uses "no manner of speaking that is not in common human usage [*in consuetudine humana*]" (DT 1.23). From this we might conclude that Augustine views the Scriptures themselves as operating is a realm of common sense, adopting a form of communication which reaches the common person. Finally, apart from patience and perseverance, Augustine demands nothing more from his readers than their acceptance of the word of God as true. This is the common faith of a Christian believer. The Scriptures are the unerring word of God, a source which cannot be contradicted, though its meaning may require examination.[46]

Concerning the content covered in these four books, the questions identified by Merriell loom large. Book 1 is concerned largely with countering Arian arguments which use Scripture to imply the subordination of the Son. Augustine counters this position with an entirely scriptural argument, developing a rule for interpreting the Biblical texts so that apparently subordinationist texts are taken to refer to Jesus in his humanity. Books 2–3 are concerned with a reading of Old Testament theophanies. Augustine is seeking to preserve the unity of operation of the three persons in the Old Testament through his insistence that these theophanies not be read as Trinitarian revelations, contrary to the approach of many of the other Church Fathers. However, in Book

4 he explores the individual missions of the Son and the Spirit to display their distinctive roles in the economy of salvation. He includes in this his first treatment of the *filioque* (DT 4.29). Throughout this his approach is entirely scriptural.

Book 4 ends with a reference to the contents of the next book where "we shall see with the Lord's help what sort of subtle crafty arguments the heretics [i.e. Arians] bring forward and how they can be demolished" (DT 4.32). It is an interesting, even surprising, observation because Augustine has already spent considerable time and energy refuting these same heretics in Book 1. But the rules have shifted, from the realm of a scripturally informed common sense, to a philosophically informed realm of theory: "From now on I will be attempting to say things that cannot altogether be said as they are thought by a man" (DT 5.1).

The Realm of Theory—Books 5–7

The first thing that may strike the reader of Books 5–7 is that the flood of scriptural texts apparent in Books 1–4 dries up to a trickle. The "subtle crafty arguments" of the heretics now considered are not scriptural, but philosophical. The terms substance, essence, person, accident and relation begin to dominate the discussion. Augustine introduces the ten Aristotelian predicates (DT 5.2); he struggles with the distinction between *ousia* and *hypostasis* (DT 5.10); he questions the validity of the term *persona* to designate that which is distinct in the Trinity (DT 5.10, 7.7); he explores whether *persona* is a genus or a species (DT 7.7–11). We have clearly moved into a realm of technical, theoretical meaning. Of course it is not as if Scripture is completely absent, but now it is a source of dilemmas that arise because of a shift from common sense to theoretical meaning.

As regards the content, the same issues, which are raised in Books 1–4, are again treated in these books, but now from a theoretical perspective. As do the Cappadocians, Augustine introduces the notion of relations as a way of distinguishing the persons of the Trinity, while preserving the divine unity. This pushes him to introduce the *filioque* as a way to distinguish the Spirit from the Son (DT 5.12–15). He even edges towards a solution to the problem of the distinct actions of the persons in relation to creation. In the concluding section of Book 5

Augustine explores the question of the way in which God relates to the created order—in order to deal with the more specific Trinitarian question one must first master the more general question of God in relation to creation. The solution that emerges is remarkably similar to what Lonergan calls contingent predication: "when he is called something with reference to creation, while indeed he begins to be called it in time, we should understand that this does not involve anything happening to God's own substance, but only to the created thing to which the relationship predicated of him refers" (DT 5.17). Lonergan scholars will know that Lonergan adopts this same approach to speak of the ontological constitution of Christ (2002, 113–5, 131–133). Lonergan rejects any analogy drawn from a finite metaphysics, for example, Rahner's notion of quasi-formal causality.

Books 6–7 deal with a problem that arises in the shift from the realm of common sense to the realm of theory. Scripture states things which may be 'appropriate' in the realm of common sense, but which are more problematic in the shift to the realm of theory. The text which grips Augustine's concerns is 1 Cor 1:24, "Christ, the power of God and the wisdom of God." Augustine is well aware that the terms power and wisdom are essential terms, that is, they refer to the divine essence. If this is the case, how then can they be predicated of the Son? In the terms of later scholasticism he is dealing with the problem of appropriation. In this context he also makes the suggestion that just as it is 'appropriate' to speak of the Son as Wisdom, so to it is 'appropriate' to speak of the Spirit as Love (DT 7.6). Still a large part of Book 7 (DT 7.7–11) is given over to a highly theoretical discussion of the notion of person in terms of genus and species. Augustine was far more aware of the difficulties associated with the word, indeed with any word, which is used to designate that which is distinct in the Trinity, than were the Cappadocians. Indeed many modern theologians could learn from Augustine on this matter, since many modern theologians seem to use the term person more as an attribute of being. This position is common among the "social Trinitarians" such a Moltmann and Volf. In doing so they inevitably display a tendency towards tritheism.

The Realm of Interiority—Books 8–11

Just about every structural analysis of *De Trinitate* notes that Book 7 marks some type of conclusion to one aspect of Augustine's project and Book 8 the beginning of a new phase. Augustine himself signals this when he challenges us to "turn our attention to the things we are going to discuss in a more inward manner than the things that have been discussed above, though in fact they are the same things" (DT 8.1). Some commentators will speak of this is the beginning of a neo-Platonic process of ascent, taking us inward and upward. However, this is just a descriptive category. In more explanatory language Augustine is inviting us into the realm of interiority. The four books that follow, Books 8–11, are a most demanding and exacting exploration of the interior realm. The trickle of scriptural quotes now evaporates leaving small pools of references that rarely relate to Trinitarian issues, but are more often words of encouragement, or symbols of the quest one has entered.

Book 8 serves as a general and gentle introduction into the realm of interiority inviting the reader to reflect on the experience of truth: "Come, hold it in that first moment in which so to speak you caught a flash ... when the word 'truth' was spoken" (DT 8.3).[47] Is Augustine here alluding to the flash of insight? He reminds the readers of their various judgments of value and invites them to explore the interior ground of these judgments (DT 8.4–5). He makes an initial exploration of the interrelationship of knowledge and love (DT 8.5). He alerts the reader to the constant self-presence of the mind: "What after all is so intimately known and so aware of its own existence as that by which things enter into our awareness, namely the mind?" (DT 8.9) He introduces the first of many "trinities," "the lover, what is being loved and love" and concludes that though we have not yet found what we are looking for "we have found where to look for it" (DT 8.14).

Book 9 begins in earnest to find some image of the Trinitarian God in the inner human being. He turns aside the "trinity" of lover, loved and love, because in the case of self-love it collapses into a binity. In its place he develops the analogy of the mind, its self-knowledge and its self-love (DT 9.3–5). Focusing on the self-knowledge of the mind, he describes it in terms of the production of an inner word. This inner word becomes the primary analogue for the procession of the

Word from the Father. Augustine further seeks to qualify the nature
of this word: it expresses "approval or disapproval," i.e. a judgment
of value (DT 9.12); to do with practical action "either for sinning or
for doing good" (DT 9.13), it is like uttering a definition (DT 9.15)
Finally it is "knowledge with love": "The kind of word then that
we are now wishing to distinguish and propose is 'knowledge with
love.' So when the mind knows and loves itself, its word is joined to
it with love. And since it loves knowledge and knows love, the word
is in the love and the love is in the word and both in the lover and
the utterer" (DT 9.15). In all this Augustine is inviting us to push
our own experience to its absolute limits. Knowledge is by a form of
identity: "this knowledge is its word in such as way that it matches it
exactly and is equal to it and identical … what is begotten is equal to
the begetter" (DT 9.16). The more perfect the knowledge the more
perfect the identity between the knowledge and what is known. In
God this becomes an identity of substance.

We can see in this that Augustine is now dealing with the very same
question that we find in the other two realms, that of the substantial
unity of the divinity, but now from the perspective of interiority.
Similarly, Augustine raises the question of the distinction of the Holy
Spirit from the Son (DT 9.17). Within the realm of interiority this
becomes the question of the relationship between knowledge and love.
Already Augustine has drawn on what has been axiomatic for him,
"nothing is loved which is not known." Now he begins to question
that axiom. He identifies an inquisitiveness, an appetite for finding
out, which precedes knowledge. This inquisitiveness "does not indeed
appear to be the love with which what is known is loved …yet it is
something of the same kind … this same appetite becomes love of
the thing known" (DT 9.18). This observation poses a problem for
Augustine which he spends most of Book 10 seeking to resolve.[48]

As I argued in the previous chapter, Book 10 presents us with a
very precise and accurate phenomenology of consciousness. The
first two chapters of Book 10 are then taken up with an analysis
of the problem identified at the end of Book 9. Augustine seeks to
prove that in every case this preceding desire is itself a love based on
knowledge. After satisfying himself that this is the case when dealing with external realities, he turns his attention to the question of

the mind and its self-knowledge and self-love, to see if "some new issue" might appear (DT 10.4). In seeking to address this question Augustine develops his phenomenology of consciousness (*mens*)[49] or "self-presence," since "nothing can be more present to it [the mind] than itself" (DT 10.5).

In modern terms Augustine is asking about the problem of "introspection." It is often expressed in terms of an ocular analogy. How can the looker look at herself while looking at something else? If our attention is focused on the object, we can only look at ourselves by ceasing to look at it. Yet Augustine rejects any similarity with ocular experience (DT 10.5). Rather the mind knows itself in the very act of knowing. This self-knowledge arises not by withdrawal from its object as proposed by Plotinus, but through a special act of intention, or heightening of consciousness, which grasps the presence of the subject in the very act of its knowing the object. As Augustine states it, the mind "should not start looking for itself as though it had drawn off from itself, but should draw off what it has added to itself" (DT 10.11). It is clear from this account that Augustine had a very clear grasp of the facts of consciousness, a clear mastery of the realm of interiority.[50]

In light of the achievements of Book 9 and 10, I must say I find Book 11 a bit of an anti-climax. It is not clear to me, at least, what Augustine is seeking to achieve in this Book. He is still in interior mode, with a consideration of various "trinities" in the operation of the mind, but the link with sensory experience muddies the waters somewhat. It may be that he is backing off from the heights of the previous two books to offer his readers something more accessible. At the end of Book 10 he offers something to "those who are slower on the uptake" (DT 10.19), but overall I think it adds little to his argument.

The Transcendent Realm—Book 12–15

While older analyses tend to place Books 12–15 together with Books 8–11, I would argue that something very different is happening here. Certainly any analysis that suggests that these books are concerned with the use of human reason to understand or supplement belief is misplaced. A significant indicator is the renewed interest Augustine shows in the Scriptures.[51] Almost absent from Books 8–11, the Scriptures now come flooding back into the text. However, their deployment is very different from the first four books where Augustine is seeking to expound and defend Christian faith from the Scriptures. Here Augustine is using the Scriptures in a more meditative and contemplative manner, bringing us back into the drama of human salvation and God's saving actions.

While Augustine has explored several trinities in the books prior to Book 12, none attains the "image of God" which he is seeking. Indeed the phrase "image of God" becomes a heart beat in Book 12, used over forty times, as Augustine explores the meaning of Genesis 1:28 and the impact that the fall of human beings has made in God's image in them. Sin undermines the image of God and turns the soul away from the eternal unchanging realm to the changeable, temporal world of the senses. The image of God "can only be preserved when facing him from whom its impression is received" (DT 12.16). In this Book Augustine is inviting the reader to move beyond the realm of interiority per se and into the realm where God is known and loved. He is concerned not with knowledge but wisdom, the "contemplation of eternal things" (DT 12.22): "And what among eternal things is more excellent than God whose nature alone is unchangeable? And what is worship of him but the love of him by which we now desire to see him, and believe and hope that we will see him?" (DT 12.22) There is an ascent here, but not the ascent of neo-Platonic achievement restricted to the few. It is an ascent born of Christian faith, hope and love, of God's love poured into our hearts, the work of divine grace.

Book 13 reinforces the invitation to the transcendent realm through a reflection on the human desire for happiness (DT 13.6–9), to conclude that the truly happy person "will not want to live a bad life in that bliss, nor will he want anything that he lacks, nor will be lack anything that he wants. Whatever he loves will be there, and he will not desire anything that is not there. Everything that is there will be good, and the most high God will be the most high good, and will be available for the enjoyment of his lovers, and thus total happiness will be forever assured" (DT 13.10). Still the shadow that hangs over our possibility of happiness is death, and so our immortality becomes a condition for the possibility of human happiness. And to win for us the possibility of immortality, the Word became flesh and dwelt among us, "For surely if the Son of God by nature became son of man by mercy for the sake of the sons of men ... how much easier it is to believe that the sons of men by nature can become sons of God by grace and dwell in God; for it is in him alone and thanks to him alone that they can be happy, by sharing in his immortality; it was to persuade us of this that the Son of God came to share in our mortality" (DT 13.12). He then proceeds to give a long and detailed account of the process of salvation, for those who question why God chose this way to save human beings (DT 13.13–23). The purpose here is, I think, more doxological than apologetic or dogmatic. Augustine is inviting us to give praise to God for the work achieved in the death and resurrection of Jesus. It is a "demonstration of how much value God put on us and how much he loved us" (DT 13.13). And our response is to be drawn into the realm in which God is known and loved.

At the end of Book 13 Augustine is still adamant that he has not yet found the image of God that he is seeking. He continues his search in earnest in Book 14 with the immediate reminder that true human wisdom is "the true and principal worship of God" (DT 14.1), the "knowledge of divine things" (DT 14.3). Again Augustine considers and rejects several proposals, including revisiting his explorations of Book 10. However some sort of climax is reached when Augustine declares that the image of God is not to be found in remembering, knowing and loving self, but rather in remembering, knowing and loving God: "This trinity of the mind is not really the image of God because the mind remembers and understands and loves itself, but because it is also able to remember and understand and love him by whom it was made. And when it does this it becomes wise ... Let it them remember its God to whose image it was made, and understand and love him. To put it in a word, let it worship the uncreated God" (DT 14.15). Again we witness Augustine inviting the reader to enter into the realm of transcendence. Still the resulting image of God only comes to complete perfection in the perfect vision of God: "From this is it clear that the image of God will achieve its full likeness of him when it attains to the full vision of him" (DT 14.24).

As Merriell has noted of Book 15, it is wrong "to dismiss it as nothing more than a summary of the preceding books plus a concluding evaluation that gives a sceptical verdict on the entire enterprise of books 8 to 14" (Merriell 1990, 30). Two thirds of the book are taken up with renewed accounts of the procession of the Word and the Spirit. Is Augustine simply repeating the material of Book 9 with some additional observations and nuances? One clear difference between this material and that of Book 9 is the presence of countless scriptural references. It is indicative that while references to the Johannine prologue abound in Book 15, there is not a single reference to it in Book 9, despite its obvious possibilities in discussing the procession of the Word in that Book. I do not think it is stretching things too far to suggest that in this Book Augustine is making connections between his exploration in the interior realm and fundamental Christian religious experience, mediated through the Scriptures. We are to "seek his face evermore" (DT 15.2—Ps 105.3).[52] Now the proceeding Word is not just any word, but the "Yes, yes; no, no" of the Father (Mt 5:37, 2 Cor 1:19–20; Jas 5:12), a Word which is "truly truth," a transcendent affirmation of being (DT 15.23). Similarly the Holy Spirit: "So it is God the Holy Spirit proceeding from God who fires man to love God and neighbour when he has been given to him, and he himself is love" (DT 15.31). This gift, which "fires man to love God," is transcendent value, value beyond all criticism, the experience of which "is the basic fulfilment of our conscious intentionality" (Lonergan 1972, 105). Again we find ourselves drawn into the realm of transcendence. Indeed these four books of *De Trinitate* are the appropriate response to the criticism made by Gunton of Augustine's theology that Trinitarian theology should be more doxological (1990, 34). These four books are in fact doxological in nature.

The *Filioque* in the Different Realms of Meaning

I would like now to return to the question of the distinction between the Word and the Spirit. As Merriell notes it is a recurring question throughout *De Trinitate*—why is the Spirit not a second Son? How is his procession different from that of the Son? A key element in Augustine's response is the *filioque*, which draws the Son into the procession of the Spirit. In order to further the thesis that Augustine has written *De Trinitate* around four distinct realms of meaning, I examine how this question appears in each realm and finds some resolution within that realm. The treatment will be fairly summary, but I hope it will help illustrate the differences between the realms as they handle a single problem.

Realm of Common Sense

As I argue above, the first four books of *De Trinitate* represent an exploration of various questions within the realm of a scripturally informed common sense. On my reading the first treatment of the *filioque* occurs in DT 4.29. Augustine here presents an argument in terms of the text of John 20:22, "Receive the Holy Spirit" where the resurrected Jesus breathes forth the Spirit. He describes this as "a convenient symbolic demonstration that the Holy Spirit proceeds from the Son as well as from the Father" (DT 4.29). He reinforces this by reference to John 15:26, "Whom I will send from the Father" and John 14:26, "Whom the Father will send in my name." Within the realm of the meaning in which he is operating, this is sufficient for Augustine to draw the conclusion that the Spirit proceeds from the Father and the Son.

Realm of Theory

Here the question takes on a different slant. Augustine has introduced us to the notions of person, relation, substance and essence. In DT 5.12–16 he teases out the distinction between the Spirit and the Son. In particular in DT 5.13 he notes the asymmetry of the relationships between the Spirit and the Father and Son, compared with the relationship between the Father and the Son: "We say the Holy Spirit of the Father, but we do not reverse it and say the Father of the Holy Spirit, or then we should take the Holy Spirit to be his son. Again we say the Holy Spirit of the Son, but we do not say the Son of the Holy Spirit, or we should take the Holy Spirit to be his father." The relationship of Father and Son already specifies the personal identity of both Father and Son. If we say, "Father of the Holy Spirit," we either over-specify the Father or under-specify the Spirit and make him indistinguishable from the Son or a second Son. None of these options Augustine finds acceptable. His solution is to implicate the Son in the procession of the Spirit: "We must confess that the Father and the Son are the origin of the Holy Spirit; not two origins, but just as the Father and Son are one God, and with reference to creation one creator and one lord, so with reference to the Holy Spirit they are one origin; but with reference to creation Father, Son and Holy Spirit are one origin, just as they are one creator and one lord" (DT 5.15). The argument Augustine adopts is one drawn from the realm of theory, based on personal distinctions grounded in the notion or relationship. Aquinas adopts the same solution in ST I q36, a2, where he argues that either one asserts the *filioque* as in the West, or one adopts a *spirituque*, which "no one says" (though many contemporary theologians have moved in this direction, for example David Coffey, Thomas Weinandy, Leonardo Boff, and Gavin D'Costa to name a few). Otherwise it is impossible to distinguish the Son from the Spirit.

Realm of Interiority

In the realm of interiority the question of the distinction between the Son and the Spirit emerges once again and requires yet another treatment. Now the question is dealt with not by reference to persons and their defining relations, but by reference to psychological facts. The basic psychological question which Augustine refers to as analogous to the distinction between the Son and the Spirit is that of the relationship between knowledge and love: "what I am asking is whether something can be loved which is unknown?" (DT 8.6). While he acknowledges that "something can be loved which is unknown, provided it is believed" (DT 8.6), the general principle that knowledge precedes love remains intact: "Now the mind cannot love itself unless it also knows itself. How can it love what it does not know?" (DT 9.3).

Yet at the end of Book 9 Augustine raises further questions about the interrelationship of knowledge and love which cast doubt over this stance. He identifies an appetite or desire for knowledge which precedes knowledge which "does not indeed appear to be love with which what is known is loved, yet is something of the same kind" (DT 9.18). This problem is then pursued with the utmost rigour in Book 10, where having working through the case of external objects to convince us that it is impossible to love the unknown (DT 10.3), he then turns his attention to the mind itself to "see if some new issue does not arise when the mind desire to know itself" (DT 10.4).

As I have already noted this leads Augustine deep into the interior realm, as he develops a most precise phenomenology of human consciousness. What I want to draw attention to here is that what is at stake in this discussion is precisely the psychological analogy for the *filioque*, and so is the interior and analogous basis for distinguishing the Son from the Spirit.

Realm of Transcendence

Merriell notes that in Book 15 Augustine returns to the problem of the distinction between the Son and the Spirit, in particular why the Spirit is not a second Son. He suggests that Augustine is discouraged by his "repeated failure to provide an adequate solution" but then presses on to offer "a valuable solution that depends on the fundamental doctrine of the procession of the Spirit from both the Father and the Son" (Merriell 1990, 33). I do not agree with this analysis of the situation. I think Augustine has offered three different solutions in the three realms of meaning, a scripturally informed common sense, the realm of theory and the realm of interiority. It is not that these solutions fail. Indeed they have become part of the classical Western approach to the theology of the Spirit. However, they are not where Augustine wants his reader to end up. Augustine the theologian never ceases to be Augustine the bishop concerned with the spiritual life of his readers. And so the question must also be pursued in the realm of transcendence.

Now in terms of the realm of transcendence, Augustine says many things about the Holy Spirit. In particular he speaks about the Holy Spirit as Love, the experience of transcendent value that is the fulfilment of our conscious intentionality, the gift of God's love poured into our hearts. He also reworks the problem of the *filioque* in terms similar to Book 9, though with the refinement that while the Spirit proceeds from the Father and the Son, he "proceeds from the Father *principally*" (DT 15.47). However, it seems to me that it is only towards the end of Book 15 that he attempts to deal with the problem in terms of the realm of transcendence, and basically fails:

> So then you have seen many true things and distinguished between them and the light by which you have seen them. Lift up your eyes to that light and fix them on that if you can. Thus you will see how the birth of the Word of God differs from the procession of the gift of God; which is the reason why the only-begotten Son said that the Holy Spirit proceeds from the Father, not that he was begotten

of him; otherwise he would be his own brother. And hence while the Spirit of them both is a kind of consubstantial communion of Father and Son, he is not (it is just unthinkable) called the Son of them both. But you are unable to fix your gaze there in order to observe this clearly and distinctly. You cannot do it, I know. I am telling the truth, I am telling it to myself, I know what I cannot do. (DT 15.50)

Augustine has sought a solution in the transcendent realm, but admits his own failure to carry through to a proper conclusion. In the light of this failure Augustine reverts back to his psychological analogy: "There is suggested a certain difference between birth and procession, because to observe by thought is not the same thing as to desire or even to enjoy by will; that all this is so, let him note and discern who can" (DT 15.50).

Conclusion

The aim of this chapter has been to present a structural analysis of Augustine's *De Trinitate* using Lonergan's notions of realms of meaning. I believe that the above analysis is, at the least, suggestive and helpful in understanding why themes recur in so many different contexts throughout the work. The suggestion is not, of course, that Augustine has something like Lonergan's realm of meaning in mind, or even that he deliberately structured his work in the way I have suggested. The structure is, I suggest, "natural" in the sense that it follows the unfolding exigencies of the mind to ask questions and order thought. But in doing so I would suggest that Augustine has anticipated Lonergan's realms of meaning by several centuries. For those who might be concerned with the validity of using a modern hermeneutic to such an ancient text, it is an intriguing question to ask whether Lonergan had Augustine's *De Trinitate* in mind when he wrote about the realms of meaning. Lonergan's thought was steeped in the tradition of Augustine and Aquinas and, as I have noted in the previous chapter, there are close parallels between Augustine's account of consciousness in Book 10 and the account given by Lonergan in Chapter 11 of *Insight*. That Lonergan supervised the thesis of Salvino Biolo on Augustine is indication of his familiarity with *De Trinitate*

(Biolio, 1969). Perhaps a fuller study of the relationship between Augustine and Lonergan is yet to be done.[53]

A more intriguing question is whether Augustine's precise phenomenology of consciousness would ever have occurred had he not been motivated by the Trinitarian problem. Here as elsewhere, revelation drives us toward the "turn to the subject," forcing us to explore more deeply the interior realm.[54] Revelation is culturally transformative, extending our cultural resources to encompass this interior realm and, in the case of Augustine, gain mastery over it.

A concluding comment concerns the sophistication of Augustine's work. If the above analysis is correct, then Augustine has quite carefully moved from one realm of meaning to another as he deals with his major Trinitarian questions. Lonergan would say Augustine instances a significant differentiation of consciousness. Not so many of his contemporary critics who often move indiscriminately from one realm to another, citing now Scripture, then dabbling in a little theory and finally failing to recognise the distinctive issues raised by interiority. The differentiation of consciousness so evident in Augustine is sadly lacking in his contemporary critics. Little wonder that so many have failed to understand the nature of his achievement.

Chapter 4
The Psychological Analogy
for the Trinity—
At Odds with Modernity[55]

For over one thousand years the psychological analogy for the Trinity was the highpoint of Trinitarian theological reflection in the western tradition. From its origins in Augustine's *De Trinitate,* to its systematic exploitation in Aquinas' *Summa Theologiae,* and beyond in the myriad commentators on Aquinas, the analogy provided a focal organizing principle for Western Trinitarian theology. Yet in the modern revival of Trinitarian thought, so much a feature of the twentieth century, the analogy has been increasingly marginalized and rejected by theologians in both the Protestant and Catholic traditions. It is now not uncommon to find dismissive comments about speculation on the "inner life of God" among theologians who prefer to expend their energies on how the doctrine of the Trinity relates the other mysteries of faith, such as creation, the paschal mystery or the church.

Undoubtedly this represents a massive turn around in the theological climate. Yet it is not initially clear why this turn around has come about. As we shall see below, the reasons theologians give are myriad, though their conclusions are the same, viz. the psychological analogy has had its day and we must now find alternative principles for organizing our theology of the Trinity. However, there are some who are resisting this litany, for example Anthony Kelly (1989; 1996), Anne Hunt (1998) and others in the Lonergan school who remain convinced of the contribution it can make. For example Robert Doran comments, "the works of Augustine and Aquinas, and in our time of Lonergan [on the psychological analogy] ... still represent the best Christian reflection of the *imago Dei* in the human subject" (1990, 346). My own position is that the analogy is a significant cultural achievement, in which are embedded important philosophical assumptions that largely run counter to the expectations of modernity and post-modernity.

Moreover these embedded assumptions are not incidental to the task of revelation and its theological exposition.

The structure of the chapter will then be as follows. First, I review the precedents for Aquinas' deployment of the analogy in Augustine's *De Trinitate* before considering the analogy in the setting of the *Summa Theologiae*, to uncover its structure and its role within Aquinas' work. I then document some of the litany of objections and rejections that the analogy has faced from theologians in the twentieth century. Next, I explore the principles embedded within the analogy and the ways in which they run counter to modernity and post-modernity. Lastly I attempt to locate the analogy within a larger cultural role for revelation and theology.

The Precedents for the Analogy in Augustine

While in his early writings Augustine explores a number of analogies for the Trinity, drawing on neo-Platonic notions of emanations, the definitive breakthrough for all future developments occurs in *De Trinitate*. Evoking the biblical theme of human beings made in the image and likeness of God, Augustine turns to an interior mode of exploration to find images of the Trinity within the human mind or consciousness (DT 8.1). In doing so he presents his readers within an almost bewildering variety of analogies, over twenty, particularly in Book 11 (LaCugna 1993, 107 n.53). This plurality is indicative of the experimental and exploratory nature of his work.

Most commentators are aware of the analogy developed at the end of Book 10 (DT 10.17), that is, of the triad of memory, understanding and will. However, it is not this analogy that will prove most effective in the Western tradition, at least in this form of expression. One difficult lies in the first element of the triad, memory. For most modern and even earlier authors, memory connotes at least some element of imagination. Memory involves eliciting images, sound, smells and other sensations from the past. Yet this connotation is explicitly excluded by Augustine, who focuses our attention on memory as a storehouse of "intelligible things" (DT 15.43). Also Biolo argues that memory relates to the primitive self-presence of the subject. Thus, given the strictures identified by Augustine, memory is the primitive self-presence of an intellectual consciousness (Biolo 1979). This precise technical meaning has been lost on most readers. The second difficulty lies in a reading of this triad as referring to potencies or faculties of the soul. At times Augustine may sound as if this is the basis for his analogy, but when he speaks with more precision it is clear that he is concerned not with faculties of the soul but with their acts, and the interrelationship of these acts. Thus, when he speaks of understanding as the second element of the analogy he arrives at the more precise formulation: "Again it is true that man's understanding, *which is formed in memory by directing thought onto it when what is known is uttered, and which is an inner word* of no particular language, has in its enormous inequality some kind of likeness to the Son" (DT 15.43) [emphasis added]. In light of these, though the formulation is different, Augustine seems to identify the triad of memory, understanding and will with the more detailed exposition given in Book 9.

In fact what proves decisive for the trajectory of the Western tradition is the analogy which Augustine works out in some detail in Book 9, to which he returns in Book 15. I have already presented some of the particulars of this analogy in the previous chapter, so I will not repeat them here. There are, however, some things I would now like to note. Firstly, Augustine is appealing to common human experience. He draws on various examples, which we have all experienced, in developing his understanding of the procession of the word: it expresses "approval or disapproval," i.e. a judgment of value (DT 9.12); it is to do with practical action "either for sinning or for doing good" (DT 9.13); it is like uttering a definition (DT 9.15). He is inviting us to attend to our own conscious experience of such acts. Secondly, the fluidity of these examples indicates once more the experimental nature of his work. He is exploring possibilities and inviting his readers to join him in the exploration. We do not yet have a formal system in place, though the elements for system are emerging. Finally, Augustine is well aware of the limitations of the analogy. He clearly recognizes the dangers of a modalist reading of the analogy (DT 15.43), but in the end it is only an analogy and so must break down at some point.

The Place of the Analogy in Aquinas' Theology

It is interesting now to compare the place of the psychological analogy in the writings of Augustine and of Aquinas. In the work of Augustine it appears in the course of a long and detailed investigation of the doctrine of the Trinity. It is a theological experiment, an exploration, based on the biblical notion of human beings made in the image and likeness of God. Without clear precedents Augustine proposes a number of analogies, playing with the themes of mind, memory, knowledge and love. While acknowledging the inadequacy of his attempts, still one senses that Augustine appreciates the significance of the breakthrough he has obtained in developing these analogies.

With Aquinas we find the analogy not as an element that emerges within a long investigation, but at the very beginning of his analysis of the triune God (ST I q27 a1). From that point on he will repeatedly turn to the analogy in his handling of the question, articles and objections raised on Trinitarian matters. It has become the key with which to explicate the mystery of the Trinity. Explicit reference to the analogy can be found in a large number of questions and articles: q27 a1–4; q28 a1 ad 4, a4 ad 1; q30 a2; q33 a3 ad1; q34, a1–3; q35 a2; q36 a1–2; q37 a1; q38 a1; q41 a6; q42 a5; q43 a5. The point of this exercise is to remind us just what a comprehensive role the analogy plays in the organization of Aquinas' theology of the Trinity.

If one may draw a parallel with the physical sciences, the difference between these two thinkers is like the difference between chemistry before and after the discovery of the periodic table of elements by Mendeleev during the 1860s. Before that time, chemistry was a series of unrelated insights seeking cohesion within a unified view. After the discovery of the periodic table, the science of chemistry began in earnest. The table became the key for the complete systematisation of chemistry. So too with the psychological analogy. Prior to its emergence in Augustine's *De Trinitate* the theology of the Trinity was largely a series of unrelated insights seeking cohesion within a unified view. In the systematics of Aquinas' *Summa Theologiae*, however, that unified view is fully in possession. Still chemistry has not yet turned its back on the periodic table of elements, while the twentieth century has witnessed a massive turning away from the psychological analogy.

The basis for the analogy is spelt out in the articles of ST I q27. Aquinas seeks analogies in the created order for the divine processions. He claims these are best found in the intellect where "the action … remains in the intelligent agent" (ST I q27 a1). This action "is to be understood by way of an intelligible emanation [*emanatio intelligibilis*]" (ST I q27 a1). The concept that is formed by this intelligible emanation results in an identity between the knower and the known, "since the intellect by the very act of understandings is made one with the object understood" (ST I q27 a1). This identity implies that the procession of the concept proceeds "by way of similitude, inasmuch as the concept of the intellect is a likeness of the object conceived" (ST I q27 a2). In God this similitude is perfect, so that the concept or Word is nothing less than God. This is the psychological equivalent of the *homoousios*.

Article 3 takes up the question as to whether there is a second procession apart from that of the word. Here Aquinas identifies another procession, "the operation of the will within ourselves involves also another procession, that of love, whereby the object loved is in the lover." While intellect and will are one in God, still the analogy recognizes a "certain order" between the procession of Word and Spirit, since "nothing can be loved by the will unless it is conceived in the intellect." Further "love requires by its very nature that it proceed only from the concept of the intellect" (ST I q27 a3). This procession however is not one of similitude "but by way of impulse and movement towards an object" which conforms us to the object loved (ST I q27 a4).

While the analogy plays a continuing role throughout the treatise on the Trinity, the next concentrated reference occurs in ST I q34–36, on the Son and Spirit. In ST I q34, a1 Aquinas expands on what he has previously said about the procession of the word. He repeats several times that the word proceeds from the intellect as a concept proceeds from understanding, not a searching for truth but as it "attains to the form of truth." This link with truth raises the possibility that the procession of the word is analogous to the procession of a judgment of truth, the "Yes" which affirms actual existence.

Question 36 returns to the procession of love as analogous to the Holy Spirit. In ST I q36 a2, he uses the psychological analogy to ground an understanding of the *filioque* since "love must proceed from a word. For we do not love anything unless we apprehend it by a mental conception." This is taken up again in ST I q43 a5 ad 2 where Aquinas qualifies the procession of the word in the following terms: "Thus the Son is sent not in accordance with every and any kind of intellectual perfection, but according to the intellectual illumination which breaks forth into the affection of love," a "Word" which "breathes forth love [*verbum spirans amorem*]." Such a word might be construed as analogous to a judgment of actual value that releases the responsible ecstasy of love (Lonergan 1985, 93).

The history of interpretation of the analogy has been tortuous to say the least, and can be traced through the text and footnotes of Lonergan's *Verbum: Word and Idea in Aquinas* (1997, passim). Principle difficulties in that history have been the inability of interpreters to distinguish processions in intellect from those in the imagination, and Scotus' inversion of the relationship between understanding and concepts. Both these stances threaten to reduce the personal procession of the Word to a pre-personal form of causation, which is inadequate to the realm of the divine. In some ways we could say that some elements of Augustine's *De Trinitate* have proved unhelpful in that the multiple analogies he develops, particularly in Book 11, often contain references to the imagination. The interpretation of Aquinas given above has been guided by Lonergan's writings in this regard.

The presuppositions of the analogy are in themselves hardly surprising. God knows and loves Godself. Is there a relationship between this self-knowledge and love and the processions spoken of in the traditional symbols of faith? There is a significant shift in horizon from the more interior formulations of Augustine to the more precise metaphysical analysis of Aquinas. Still neither the more interior approach nor the more technical one has found a home in twentieth century thought on the Trinity. It is now time to consider these modern objections.

The Modern Litany against the Analogy

As one might expect there has been a significant rejection of the analogy from Protestant theologians who find it difficult to derive from the Biblical witness.

For Karl Barth the whole project of *vestigia trinitatis*, of which the psychological analogy is for Barth simply another example, is suspect because it threatens to replace or undermine the single "root" of the doctrine of the Trinity, that is, "the Biblical concept of revelation [which] itself the root of the doctrine of the Trinity" (1936, 1/1: 383–84). Given the approach of the *vestigia trinitatis*, "the idea of a second root of the doctrine of the Trinity was bound to assert itself. It might then be supposed that fundamentally the Trinity could just as well be derived from and grounded upon human self-consciousness ... as from Holy Scripture" (ibid. 393). Barth does not doubt the good will of those Church Fathers who sought such analogies. "The inventors of the *vestigia trinitatis* had no wish to produce a second and different root of the doctrine of the Trinity parallel to revelation ... But their action is deeply overshadowed by the question whether nevertheless this is not precisely what they have done" (ibid. 396). Such a project lies under the general suspicion with which Barth holds all attempts at a natural theology of God, which he calls the *analogia entis*.

Moltmann takes a different tack. While not explicitly mentioning the psychological analogy he criticizes the approach of Aquinas, and the Western tradition in general, for its starting point in *De Deo uno*. This leads to the "general conception of the absolute subject" and the Trinity "viewed as an eternal process of self-differentiation and self-identification of the absolute subject." Such an approach "leads unintentionally but inescapably to the reduction of the doctrine of the Trinity to monotheism" (1981, 17), by which Moltmann means modalism.

This suspicion of modalism is also implied by Wolfhart Pannenberg and Colin Gunton. For Pannenberg, "[for] all the differentiation in the self-consciousness, the God of this understanding is a single subject ... Attempts to find self-subsistent relations for the Son and Spirit rather than relations merely in the Father remained artificial in the context of the psychological analogy" (1991, 1:295). Pannenberg also seems to accept the critique of Spinoza, that "[if] we ascribe will and intellect to God, they have to be so totally different from ours that they have no more than the name in common" (ibid. 375), so there can be no real basis for any psychological analogy.

Gunton pushes the matter further. For Gunton, Augustine's psychological analogy has left the West with a "baneful legacy," the twin blights of individualism and intellectualism: "I want to suggest that the problem with the trinitarian analogies as Augustine presents them is that they impose upon the doctrine of the Trinity a conception of the divine threeness which owes more to neoplatonic philosophy than to the triune economy, and that the outcome is, again, a view of an unknown substance *supporting* the three persons rather than *being constituted* by their relatedness. The true ontological foundations of the doctrine of the Trinity, that is to say, are to be found in the conception of a threefold mind and not in the economy of salvation" (Gunton 1997, 42–43). Thus Augustine's analogies have precipitated a theological crisis in the Western tradition which must now be overcome, generally through an excavation of the resources of Eastern Orthodox approaches to the Trinity.

While we might expect to find a more sympathetic approach from Catholic authors, this is, with some few exceptions, not the case.

Karl Rahner is undoubtedly a key figure in the revival among Catholic theologians of Trinitarian theology in the twentieth century. Yet his approach to the psychological analogy is lukewarm to say the least. He expresses serious reservations about its logic: "it postulates *from* the doctrine of the Trinity a model of human knowledge and love, which either remains questionable, or about which it is not clear that it can be more than a *model* of human knowledge as *finite*. And this model it applies again to God ... it becomes clear too that such a psychological theory of the Trinity has the character of what the other sciences call an 'hypothesis'" (1974, 117–18; also 1982, 135–36). For Rahner, the analogy is a hypothesis drawn from a model of human knowledge, where the model itself is drawn from belief about the Trinity. There is a circularity to this procedure which renders it of questionable value. He also points out that "when developing its ideas it has, as it were, forgotten about the 'economic' Trinity" (ibid. 44) (Rahner in particular levels this charge at the work of Lonergan). As an alternative Rahner proposes a fourfold group of aspects: "(a) Origin-Future; (b) History-Transcendence; (c) Invitation-Acceptance; (d) Knowledge-Love"(ibid. 88), a proposal which has found little resonance in contemporary writings. Drawing his inspiration from Rahner, David Coffey dismisses the analogy as a mere illustration, hardly worthy of theology at all (1979, 11–32; 1999, 4).

Similarly, Walter Kasper, in his magisterial work *The God of Jesus Christ,* shows scant interest in the psychological analogy, referring briefly to Thomas Aquinas as "showing very great courage" in describing the procession of the Word as an "intellectual emanation" (1984,

187). Why this required "great courage" is not explained, nor does the analogy play any further role in Kasper's discussion.

Hans Urs von Balthasar has been particular scathing of the approach of the psychological analogy.[56] According to Hunt, Balthasar "eschews a consideration of human consciousness as primary analogy for the Trinity of divine persons, and is deeply suspicious of any kind of turn to the subject." Balthasar rejects any analogy based on "the human mind and its acts of intellect and will" since "both processions must be understood as processions of love." As Hunt comments, there is a real danger of voluntarism in Balthasar's position (Hunt 1988, 200). For Balthasar, "only love is credible." In its place Balthasar seeks to find analogies for the Trinity in the paschal mystery, in the death, descent into hell and resurrection of the Son.

Finally, we turn to the work of Catherine LaCugna. For LaCugna, the whole movement from God-for-us in the economy of salvation (*oikonomia*) towards God-in-Godself (*theologia*), as found in Augustine and Aquinas in the West and Gregory of Palamas in the East, marks the "defeat" of the doctrine of the Trinity. And of course, the psychological analogy is the culmination of that process of defeat, at least in the Western tradition. LaCugna questions whether "postulating an ontologically distinct 'intradivine' realm of processions, relations, and persons [is] a necessary part of trinitarian doctrine." If it is, then there is an inevitable split between *oikonomia* and *theologia*. "If not, then the unity of *oikonomia* and *theologia*, as well as the equality of the divine persons, must be maintained on other grounds, without appeal to the transeconomic realm" (LaCugna 1993, 12–13).

Lest this rejection seem total I should draw attention to the positive treatment of the analogy in Anthony Kelly's work, *The Trinity of Love*. Kelly not only gives a positive account of the analogy in his presentation of the thought of Aquinas (1989, 115–38), he also seeks to develop a modern appropriation of the analogy for the present day (ibid. 139–73). Also the works by Mary Anne Fatula, *The Triune God of Christian Faith* (1990, 68), Gerald O'Collins, *The Tripersonal God: Understanding and Interpreting the Trinity* (1999, 135–37, 144–45), and William Hill, *The Three-Personed God* (1982, 55–56, 73–78) give an exposition of the analogy with no negative comment.

The Analogy at Odds with Modernity

It is not my intention to defend the psychological analogy against all
the charges that have been levelled against it by theologians in the
twentieth century. What I do below will address some of these criticisms indirectly, though I fear that the general suspicion of modalism
and subsequent individualism will always remain for some (Similarly,
the so-called "social analogy" will always remain suspect of tritheism).
Rather than defend the analogy in that way I prefer to identify certain
features of the analogy which run against the grain of modernity and
post-modernity. Moreover, I suggest that these features are not just
accidental to our theologizing about the Trinity but may in fact be one
element of the purpose of the revelation of the Trinity itself.

Against the linguistic turn

A key feature of the Thomistic understanding of the psychological
analogy for the procession of the Word is the relationship it expresses
between understanding and concept formation. Within the analogy,
the word proceeds as an intelligible emanation. This refers to the manner in which concepts, definitions, hypotheses and judgments emerge
from an intelligible and intelligent grasp of their intended object. The
procession is not simply caused, in an impersonal sense, but is "because."
I am able to formulate a concept because I understand. Such a form
of causation is eminently personal, not drawn from the subpersonal
realm of physical causation. Still, while it is personal it is also subject
to a certain necessity, a rational necessity. The word "must" proceed if
I am to be true to my own nature as intelligent and reasonable.

What is clearly embedded in such a position is the inherent priority
of understanding over language. This priority is entirely reversed in
the modern "turn to the linguistic." Such a linguistic turn is evident,
for example, in the theologies of George Lindbeck and John Milbank.
Lindbeck conceives of religious doctrines as a form of linguistic grammar with no necessary ontological reference (1984). Different sets of
doctrines simply represent different grammars and are basically incom-
mensurable. Lindbeck calls his approach "cultural-linguistic," which
he sets in opposition to "propositional" and "experiential-expressivist"
understandings of religious doctrines. In Lindbeck's view, religion
"functions somewhat like a Kantian a priori" not however of concepts

but a "set of acquired skills that could be different" (ibid. 33). These skills shape human subjectivity like a language or culture.

Milbank expresses his rejection of Aquinas' position most explicitly. He identifies Aquinas' "error" in the following terms: "language does not stand for ideas, as Aquinas thought, but constitutes ideas and 'expresses' things in their disclosure of truth for us" (1997, 29), though Milbank's own attempts to interpret Aquinas leave a lot to be desired (Ormerod 1999). Milbank identifies his own position as one of "linguistic idealism" (1991, 343), a position that is central to his post-modern rejection of the social sciences. Such conceptualism marks what Lonergan identifies as a "flight from understanding," a flight which in modernity has reduced reason to instrumentality and introduced a pall of suspicion over the powers of intelligence. From this perspective Milbank's option for "linguistic idealism" and the thoroughgoing historicism of post-modernity do not represent a solution to the problems posed by modernity. Rather they are the final stages of decline and dissolution of a longer cycle of decline initiated by the emergence and dominance of conceptualism since the time of Duns Scotus (the role of Scotus in this drama has been identified by Lonergan (1992, 396–97), Hans Urs von Balthasar (Doran 1998, 585-86 n.46),[57] Alasdair MacIntyre (1990, 152–53), and less explicitly by John Paul II in *Fides et Ratio* (n.45)).

These two theologians are indicative of the linguistic turn of much modern thought. They stand to Aquinas' theology much as conceptualism and nominalism stood in the intellectual decline of the Western tradition following his scholastic synthesis. From a modern perspective the psychological analogy implies a rejection of this linguistic turn and a reassertion of the role of understanding, prior to and foundational of all language. Still the implications of this priority of understanding go further than the problem of the modern linguistic turn. They also have metaphysical implications.

The implicit realism of the analogy

The next feature of the psychological analogy that I would like to highlight is the implicit realism of the analogy. This is evident in two ways. The first is the way in which the analogy understands the relationship between knowledge and reality; the second is evident in the very fact of using an analogy at all.

Knowledge and reality

Central to the analogy for the procession of the Word is the presupposition of the adequacy of knowledge to reality, an *adaequatio intellectus et rei*. The analogy is grounded in the philosophical confidence that knowledge of reality is possible. Such an *adaequatio* is not found in some sensible similarity, but in the intellect, in understanding. The product of divine understanding, the Word, is perfectly adequate to the divine reality, and so is nothing less than that divine reality itself—"the concept of the intellect is a likeness of the object conceived" (ST I q27 a2).

This confidence of the powers of the intellect to know reality has a clear metaphysical implication. If the understanding of the intellect expressed in the concept is adequate to the real, then this can only be because the real is intrinsically intelligible. If reality is not intrinsically intelligible, then the understanding of the intellect cannot be adequate to the real.

These two positions, the power of intellect to know reality and the intrinsic intelligibility of reality, stand in diametric opposition to the dominant post-Kantian epistemology of our day, which has effectively separated knowledge and reality, leading to widespread epistemological, and eventually moral, relativism. It is for this reason that Pope John Paul II made repeated calls in the encyclical *Fides et Ratio* (FR n.5, 6, 47, 56) for philosophers to recover their confidence in the powers of the intellect to understand reality, as a means of overcoming our present relativistic plight.

Analogy, not model (Kelly 1989, 118)

When contemporary authors refer to the psychological analogy they almost uniformly refer to it as the psychological model rather than an analogy (Coffey 1979, 11–31) (O'Collins 1999, 145). It is amazing how much this choice of terminology reflects a worldview at variance with that of those who first developed the analogy. The language of "models" comes from a post-Kantian epistemology which views the constructions of the mind as models which are projected onto a phenomenal world, but which never really access the noumenal "thing-in-itself." This noumena remains permanently beyond our grasp. The language of models is now widespread in the philosophy of science. For some it is simply a statement of the tentative nature of scientific hypotheses, and so not a rejection of realism. For others, such as Thomas S. Kuhn (1996), the influence of Kantian relativism is more evident. This notion of projected models/interpretations/ meanings lies at the heart of much modern relativism, where each has his or her own "interpretation" which are all equally valid because reality remains intrinsically unintelligible. As a "model" a psychological model "works" even if it never corresponds to anything "real" in human psychology.

A good example of this problem can be found in various writings of David Coffey. In seeking to revise Trinitarian theology Coffey often speaks of the "procession model," embodied in the Nicene Creed, which he conflates with the "psychological model" of Augustine and Aquinas. These he contrasts with his own "bestowal model," which involves a more complex set of inner-Trinitarian relationships. Coffey considers these two models as being based on "two irreducible Trinitarian data" so that no harmonising synthesis is necessary, or possible (1979; 1984, 470–71; 1986, 230–35; 1999a, 46–65). This could reflect a Kantian assumption that our interpretations are simply projections onto the reality of God, not genuine meanings which find their ground in that reality.

Analogy language, however, is based on an implicit realism. It seeks to compare two realities, one known, and the other relatively unknown. One reality, the human psychology of knowing and loving is expressed in either metaphysical (Aquinas) or direct interior (Augustine) language that effectively mediates the intelligible reality of those events. This reality as known is then compared with another reality, the reality of the triune God, known through Christian faith. In the case of analogy, if the analysis of the psychological reality is invalid, inaccurate or faulty, then the whole process is pointless. No analogy ensues.

Perhaps one could summarize the thrust of the above comments in the lapidary expression, "the value of rationality." The psychological analogy has deeply embedded within it the *value of human rationality*. However, it is not the conceptualist deductive rationality we commonly mean by that term. Such a conception is entirely inadequate to a proper understanding of human rationality. Rather, it is the dynamic and immanent rationality of the human subject who is governed by the transcendental precepts: Be Attentive, Be Intelligent, Be Reasonable, Be Responsible (Lonergan 1972, 20). This is the rationality of submitting oneself to the immanent norms, the inner rational necessity, of truth and goodness. This constitutes the basic meaning of the "intelligible emanation" that is so central to Aquinas' exposition of the processions of Word and Spirit.[58]

The rationality of value

So far we have considered the ways in which the psychological analogy for the procession of the Word embedded certain assumptions about understanding, knowledge and reality. It is now time to turn to the procession of the Holy Spirit, which is conceived as a procession of love. Still, it is not any procession of love, but a procession grounded in the intelligently grasped and reasonably affirmed reality of the Godhead. This affirmation includes an affirmation of the ultimate goodness of the Godhead and so grounds a responsible outpouring of ecstatic love. The assumption we find embedded in this account I would speak of as the "rationality of value." By rationality, as I noted above, I do not mean the deductive rationality of conceptualism, but the intrinsic rationality of the subject who is dynamically and consciously oriented to truth and goodness. Put simply, genuine love is grounded in truth, a constant theme of Pope John Paul II.[59]

One consequence of such a stance is that, contrary to modern and post-modern expectations, moral debates are intrinsically, that is, rationally, decidable. This is in stark contrast to our present interminable public debates on sensitive moral issues, as highlighted by MacIntyre in relation to public debate on abortion (1984, 6–22). Whereas for modernity, values are relegated to the realm of the irrational and private, the assumption of the psychological analogy is that values are "rational" and hence public. Some have argued that this stance needs to be re-inserted into our public life. For example, moral theologian David Hollenbach has argued for the virtue of "intellectual solidarity—a willingness to take other persons seriously enough to engage them in conversation and debate about what they think makes life worth living." This goes beyond mere tolerance that is a "strategy for non-interference" (Hollenbach 1994, 334). Such a position of engagement reflects the stance of the psychological analogy. Embedded within the analogy is a rejection of the moral relativism so dominant in our current modern and post-modern cultures.

The reasonableness of faith

The final presupposition that I would like to explore, which runs counter to our present age, is one of the reasonableness of Christian faith. The psychological analogy is a paradigmatic example of theology as faith seeking understanding. It is an attempt to show that at the very least, the doctrine of the Trinity is in itself not self-contradictory or completely unintelligible to the human mind. As such it does not attempt to prove the Trinity, a position Aquinas rejects as impossible outside of revelation. But it does provide a solid "plausibility structure" for the doctrine. From that perspective, it could well serve an apologetic purpose, or even assist in inter-faith dialogue (Dupuis 1997, 274–75).

Here we can contrast the theology of Aquinas, as it is grounded in the analogy, and much contemporary writing. A constant criticism made by modern authors is that the analogy does not relate the Trinity to other aspects of faith, and its concentration of the "inner life" of God is either unnecessary or simply futile. The modern approach has been rather to relate the doctrine of the Trinity to other aspects of faith, such as the paschal mystery, creation or ecclesiology and so on. Now it is clear, as Hunt rightly points out, that both tasks are appropriate and can be justified by reference to Vatican I, *Dei Filius* (1998, 214). However, to back away from the first task, of seeking the intelligibility of the doctrine in itself, can mark a retreat from a position on the inherent intelligibility of faith and a move towards fideism. Inasmuch as one moves in that direction, the first task is thought of as simply unnecessary. Inevitably, this will lead to the conclusion that Christian faith is little more than just one more religious mythology that is part of the present burgeoning religious marketplace.

Again the presupposition of most modern and post-modern culture is that religious faith is in the realm of the irrational, or at best the non-rational, something to be confined to the private world of values, not the public world of reason. In such a setting the psychological analogy asserts the publicly reasonable nature of Christian faith. A sole emphasis on relating the doctrine of the Trinity to other aspects of Christian faith can represent a capitulation to our present culture on this matter.[60]

Revelation and Culture

Underlying the above discussion is an understanding of the inter-relationship between theology, revelation and culture. I now explore the possibility of revelation being culturally transformative, using the psychological analogy as one example.

It has become commonplace in theology to speak of social sin. While recognizing the analogical use of the term "sin," the concept of social sin expresses the ways in which institutions can in their very structures pervert the human good and lead to decline. One might think, for example, of the ways in which apartheid laws institutionalized the multiple personal sins of racism in South Africa. The concept of social sin is important because it helps us recognize that these structures not only arise from human sinfulness, but in themselves they orient us away from the good by creating a social milieu in which sin is normalized. Feminist and liberation theologians have added to the notion of social sin by speaking of "ideology critique." It is not enough to change the institutions, one must also challenge the distorted meanings and values which they support, and which meanings and values in turn support those institutions.

Still the issues concerning the rationality of value and the value of rationality we have identified above are not as easily categorized, as are the ideologies of racism and patriarchy. They operate on a larger canvas, often not so clearly institutionalised, except perhaps in the academy. They may be thought to represent a deeper alienation, an alienation from our basic identity and destiny as knowers of the truth and doers of the good. This alienation is given formal expression, not so much in laws and institutions, but in the works of philosophers whose ideas shape our cultures on the time frame of centuries. Slowly these ideas move out of the minds of their creators and into the realm of our common sense. They become the air we breathe, the very fabric of our thought. We can hardly begin to think in other categories because they have shaped our thought from the cradle. As Lonergan notes, "the hopeless tangle ... of the endlessly multiplied philosophies is not merely a cul-de-sac for human progress; it is also a reign of sin, a despotism of darkness; and men are its slaves" (1958, 714). Can we not recognize in this process the notion of "cultural sin," the cumulative distortions of philosophy which alienate us from our basic identity and destiny?

The Vatican II Dogmatic Constitution of Divine Revelation, *Dei Verbum*, speaks of revelation as "for the sake of our salvation" (DV n.11). The notion of salvation is multi-layered and touches on all those aspects of human living that are distorted by human sin and evil. These clearly include personal relationships, and we now recognize the involvement of social structures in sin and evil, but the question arises as to whether the same can be said of our cultural orientations. If the notion of cultural sin is valid, then it should not be surprising if revelation were to have a salvific significance at the level of such cultural sin. Is it not possible to view the psychological analogy precisely as a theological and cultural achievement which arises under the cultural impact of the revelation of the triune God, an achievement required to overcome the multiple philosophical stances identified above? I take up this argument more fully elsewhere (Ormerod 2000, esp. 247–277).

Such a stance is the fundamental response to Rahner's concern about the circularity of the analogy. It may well be true, as Rahner claims, that our investigation of human knowing and loving is driven by our prior knowledge of processions in God. It may well be that we then apply the outcomes of this investigation to the Trinity itself. But in the process something has been gained, if the analogy stands. For we have been driven to clarify the immanent desire for truth and goodness within human consciousness, in a way that upholds our basic identity and destiny as knowers of the truth and doers of the good. And in doing so we have upheld the dignity of each and every human being as made in the image and likeness of God, so that very person, rich and poor, saint and sinner, male or female, contains in his or her inner life a faint reflection of the glory of the triune God. As Augustine states: "Therefore, if it is with reference to its capacity to use reason and understanding in order to understand and gaze upon

God that it was made to the image of God, it follows that from the moment this great and wonderful nature begins to be, this image is always there, whether it is so worn away as to be almost nothing, or faint and distorted, or clear and beautiful" (DT 14.6).

Conclusion

We may now ask what lessons we might learn from the above account of the psychological analogy and its place in the Western tradition. The first and perhaps most important is that the minimal accounts of the analogy found in much theological literature, which speaks all to quickly of "processions of knowledge and love," or the analogy of memory, understanding and will, do scant justice to the depths contained in the analogy. It is only in attention to its precise details that we can hope to uncover those depths. Such attention will not occur in a theological environment that is hostile to the analogy itself. Contemporary theologians are in great danger of locking themselves out of the riches the analogy contains because of a pre-judgment that it has nothing to offer.

Secondly, much of the criticism of the analogy flows from a very different conception of the theological project operating in the Western tradition. The analogy does not attempt to prove anything about God (*pace* Rahner), nor does it seek to provide an alternative source of information about God to revelation (*pace* Barth). It takes the basic datum of the Christian dogmatic tradition, one God, two processions and three persons, and seeks to find some analogy in the created order for making sense of such a belief. It is a paradigmatic example of "faith seeking understanding." The search for analogies in the created order is part of the common Christian heritage, both East and West. For all its power, however, the psychological analogy is simply the least worst. By grounding itself in the operations of the human spirit, it has fewer flaws than any competitor precisely because of its appeal to the immateriality of the spirit, human and divine.

Finally, the major gap between this element of the Western tradition and our present context lies not just in our conception of the theological project, but in the philosophical assumptions which underpin that project. As has been detailed above, on several major issues the psychological analogy represents an opposing position to the dominant philosophical assumptions that are part of our present cultural milieu. Such a gap can only be bridged if theologians begin to ask fundamental questions about knowing, reality and the relationship between them. These are self-transformative questions that can lead to the personal breakthrough Lonergan identified as "intellectual conversion" (1972, 238–39). This is the real power of the psychological analogy.

In his own day the psychological analogy of Aquinas represented a high point of theological speculation, encapsulating, as we have seen above, key philosophical positions within the framework of a theology of the Trinity. It is nothing less than a major cultural achievement. That it is no longer viewed as such may speak more about our own cultural malaise than of the value and significance of the analogy itself. The role of the psychological analogy in our contemporary theological setting must then be very different from its setting in Aquinas. Theology must conceive itself not simply as interpretative of past and present texts but as culturally transformative (Doran 1990, 440–70). If the analogy is to have a contemporary theological role it must clearly appropriate its own cultural depth as a critique of, and alternative to, the dominant cultural strains of modernity and post-modernity.

Chapter 5
Reappropriating the Doctrine of Appropriation

As with the psychological analogy, the Trinitarian doctrine of appropriation has been increasingly sidelined in contemporary theology as part of the general neglect of the Western tradition. The purpose of this doctrine was to be able to "say more than can be said," that is, it provided a framework either for understanding scriptural statements which might relate to the Father, Son or Spirit, but which caused problems when one moved to a more explanatory mode of thinking; or for saying more than could be justified systematically but which somehow "felt right." An example of the first might be the account of Scripture that states that Mary conceived Jesus through the "power of the Holy Spirit." To an explanatory mode of thinking, the power of the Holy Spirit is nothing more or less than the power of the Son or the power of the Father, since their power resides in the divine nature, which is common. However, we could argue that Luke is evoking the image of the spirit of God hovering over creation (Gn 1:1), and so this is not an inappropriate way of talking. Similarly we might speak, as we do in the creed, of "God the Father, almighty, maker of heaven and earth." Again in an explanatory mode, we might hold that creation is equally the task of Father, Son and Spirit, one God, as we find in the *Credo* of Paul VI. However, since the Father is the origin of both the Son and the Spirit, we get a certain sense of the rightness of speaking about the Father as creator. In this way the Western tradition sought to expand the reach of Trinitarian language beyond what could be strictly justified, in ways which remained true to Scripture and theological analogy.

Contemporary theology has in general taken a more jaundiced view of this style of theologising. While Leonardo Boff adopts the language of appropriation with little comment (1988, 97), David Coffey warns that we should hesitate to evoke it where Scripture seems to indicate an activity or role proper to a particular person (1979, 101). Denis

Edwards attempts to extend such proper roles of the individual persons into the order of creation (1995, 118ff). Catherine LaCugna argues that "the attributions often are arbitrary and sometimes contradict biblical ways of speaking about God's activity." Further, "if a theology were to start from and centre itself on the economy, all the while presupposing the essential unity of economy and 'theology', it would have no need for a doctrine of appropriations" (LaCugna 1993, 98, 100). Thomas Torrance is more blunt. Given a complete perichoretic approach to the Trinity "the so-called 'law of appropriations' brought in by Latin theology to redress an unbalanced essentialist approach to the doctrine of the Trinity from the One Being of God … falls completely away as an idea that is both otiose and damaging of the intrinsic truth" of revelation (Torrance 1996, 200).

The aim of this present chapter is to attempt a reappropriation of the theological doctrine of appropriations. I begin with an account of the classical doctrine as it emerges in the writings of Augustine's *De Trinitate* and the consider its handling in the *Summa Theologiae* of Thomas Aquinas, as well as the ways this doctrine has been "received" in more recent writings. I then attempt to recast the doctrine in terms of what Bernard Lonergan call the "functions of meaning." Finally I examine the writings of three contemporary Trinitarian theologians and suggest that their proposals for understanding of the Trinity can best be placed within this recasting of the doctrine of appropriation.

The Western Tradition on Appropriation

Though Augustine does not use the term "appropriation" in *De Trinitate*, he struggles with the basic problem in Books 6 and 7. As I have argued in Chapter 3, in this section of *De Trinitate* Augustine is seeking to transpose his account of the Trinity from a scripturally informed common sense to a philosophically informed technical language, employing such terms as essence, substance, person, and relation. This shift in the realm of meaning creates problems since things which are said, and for Augustine said truly because they are the word of God, can become problematic when we transpose them into a technical realm of meaning. The example that Augustine deals with is the teaching of Paul that "Christ [is] the power and wisdom of God" (1 Cor 1:24). Augustine is well aware that the terms power and wisdom are "essential" terms, that is, they relate to the divine essence. Thus they are in fact identical to that essence and so they are common to all three persons (DT 6.2, 7.1). If we say Christ is the power and wisdom of God, do we say that the Father is not wise with his own wisdom and powerful with his own power? Do we imply that the Spirit is not powerful or wise? Or do we say that "Christ is not the power of God and the wisdom of God, and thus shamelessly and irreligiously contradict the apostle"? (DT 7.2).

Augustine's solution is to note that while "the Father and the Son are together one being and one greatness and one truth and one wisdom," nonetheless "because wisdom is also Word, though not Word in the same way as wisdom … let us take it as being the same, when it is called Word, as if it were called 'born wisdom'" (DT 7.3). Augustine is here appealing to a type of analogous usage, which is "appropriate" while not strictly true in a restrictive or explanatory sense. What Paul is saying is true enough, but not the whole truth. Augustine will mount the same type of argument latter in Book 15 when he makes a similar case for calling the Holy Spirit love. "This, surely, is the most sensible way for us to believe or understand the matter, that the Holy Spirit is not alone in that triad in being charity, but that there is a good reason for distinctively calling him charity" (DT 15.37).

In both these cases we can see Augustine stretching the possibilities of meaning. The austerity of a purely cognitive meaning cannot do justice to the full range of what one might want to say, and say meaningfully, about the Trinity. The method of appropriation allows Augustine to affirm meanings as found in Scripture while at the same time acknowledging their limitations. The issue that confronts any application of this process, however, is how to do so without being completely arbitrary. What constitutes the "good reason" that Augustine appeals to in drawing this appropriation? The answer, in this case, is the psychological analogy.

We find further refinement of this problem in the work of Aquinas.[61] Aquinas' account of appropriation (ST I q39 a7, a8) must be read in light of his more exacting grammar of divinity and divine simplicity, established earlier in the *Summa*. Any property or attribute posited of the divine can never mean exactly what it means as applied to creatures. We know divinity only through negation, by pre-eminence or analogously. In divinity itself all attributes are equal to one another and to the divine essence. Because of this, the theory of appropriating essential attributes to individual persons cannot be seen as a back door entry into the truth of the revealed doctrine of the Trinity. The Trinity is a mystery of faith, only knowable because it is revealed (ST I q32 a1). Any attempt to derive the divine persons from essential attributes is ruled out of court.

Why then would we seek to appropriate essential attributes to individual persons? Aquinas answers, "for the *manifestation* of our faith it is fitting that the essential attributes should be appropriated to the persons" (ST I q39 a7). Aquinas seems to be suggesting that the fullness of our faith life cannot be confined with what we can strictly affirm as cognitively true. Faith requires a fuller manifestation, a fuller *intellectum fidei*, which moves beyond the limits of a purely cognitive truth, even while remaining faithful to it. In ST I q39 a7 he provides two examples of what he has in mind: "The divine person can be manifested in a twofold manner by the essential attributes; in one way by similitude, and thus the things which belong to the intellect are appropriated to the Son, Who proceeds by way of intellect, as Word. In another way by dissimilitude; as power is appropriated to the Father, as Augustine says, because fathers by reason of old age are sometimes feeble; lest anything of the kind be imagined of God." While the second of these might strike us as somewhat quaint, the first points in a more profound direction. Aquinas explicitly evokes the psychological analogy as a way of grounding the process of appropriation. Because the procession of the Word can be conceived as analogous to an intellectual emanation from understanding to conception, "things which belong to the intellect" such as wisdom, understanding and truth may be fittingly appropriated to the Son. The psychological analogy clearly provides Aquinas with one method of controlling the process of appropriation.

The following article in the *Summa*, ST I q39 a8, Aquinas provides various examples drawn from the writings of the "holy doctors," drawing on four general principles which guide the process of appropriation: "Our intellect, which is led to the knowledge of God from creatures, must consider God according to the mode derived from creatures. In considering any creature four points present themselves to us in due order. Firstly, the thing itself taken absolutely is considered as a being. Secondly, it is considered as one. Thirdly, its intrinsic power of operation and causality is considered. The fourth point of consideration embraces its relation to its effects. Hence this fourfold consideration comes to our mind in reference to God." These four points provide a road map as Aquinas works his way through the various suggestions of previous theologians, seeking to show that the process of appropriation should not be arbitrary or thoughtless, but rests on intelligent, if not absolutely necessary, reasons.

Still some of these appropriations—"eternity is in the Father, species is in the Image; and use is in the Gift" (Hilary); "unity is in the Father, equality is in the Son, and in the Holy Ghost is the concord of equality and unity" (Augustine)—do strike us as of at most marginal interest. Aquinas is being faithful to his received theological tradition, but one is left wondering if these are worth the effort of their justification. One can see why LaCugna might claim that "the attributions often are arbitrary and sometimes contradict biblical ways of speaking about God's activity" (1993, 98). Even as Aquinas remains faithful to his received tradition while transforming it, perhaps it is time to transform the traditional approach to appropriation, while still remaining faithful to its basic thrust.

The Modern Reception of Appropriation[62]

While the doctrine of appropriation sat comfortably within the Western tradition, it began to be seriously questioned in the writings of Karl Rahner. Rahner, however, shifts attention away from the question of what can be said or not said about the persons of the Trinity (the appropriation of attributes) to the actions of God in the economy of salvation. His starting point is the unity of the divine operation, expressed in terms of the traditional doctrine of works *ad extra*, that is, the divine operation "outside" God (*ad extra*) is the work of all three persons indistinguishably. However, certain works are appropriated to the Father (creation), the Son (redemption) and the Spirit (sanctification). Rahner objects that the doctrine of works *ad extra* is inadequate to account for the activity of divine self-communication, particularly for the reality of incarnation and grace which "should not be reduced to a 'relation' (a purely mental relation at that) of the one God to the elected creature, nor to a relation which is merely 'appropriated' to the other divine persons" (1974, 23). In particular, he notes that in the case of the incarnation the mission is "proper" to Logos, that is, it is "something which belongs to the Logos alone, which is the history of the one divine person, in contrast to the other divine persons" (ibid.). In this case and in the case of grace Rahner speaks of a "proper relation" to the created order as distinct from an appropriated relation.

As it stands, this position is readily acceptable within the Western tradition, perhaps more so in the case of the Incarnation than grace. For example Aquinas holds that "the whole Trinity dwells in the mind by sanctifying grace" (ST I q43 a5). His theological vision of grace includes invisible missions of both the Logos and the Spirit, with their effects modelled on the psychological analogy. However, Rahner pushes the notion further than this by his insistence that, contrary to Aquinas, only the Logos could have been incarnated. As a consequence, "what Jesus is and does as man reveals the Logos himself; it is the reality of the Logos as our salvation amidst us … here the Logos with God and the Logos with us, the immanent and the economic Logos, are strictly the same" (1974, 33). Rahner is arguing that there is something "proper" to the Logos as the immanent Word of God, which means that only the Logos could have been incarnated in the human being Jesus of Nazareth. That is, the characteristics that define the immanent identity of the Logos are such that only the Logos could assume the proper role of being incarnate. Here two meanings of the word "proper" merge. One is the proper, personal identity of persons within the Trinity; the other is the possibility of "proper" as distinct from "appropriated" roles in the economy. For Rahner these are necessarily linked. This linking is a much stronger statement than simply the question of "proper" as distinct from "appropriated" roles.

Though Rahner alludes to grace as proper to the Holy Spirit, David Coffey has given the full argument for such a position (1979; 1984; 1986). Coffey wants to speak of not only a proper role for the Spirit in the operation of grace, but more particularly of a proper mission for the Spirit in the incarnation of the Logos. There is a sense, Coffey argues, in which we can speak of the Holy Spirit as "incarnated" in the person of Jesus, since Jesus is the one conceived by the power of the Holy Spirit. Here Coffey warns that we must be slow to use the notion of appropriation when Scripture seems to imply a "proper" role (1979, 101). One implication of this proper mission, which implicates the Spirit in the Incarnation, is that we must reconceptualise the inner-Trinitarian relations to involve the Spirit in the procession of the Logos. Coffey achieves this through his adoption of the Augustinian notion of the Spirit as the mutual love between the Father and Son, while Weinandy posed a different solution to basically the same problem (1995).

While both Rahner and Coffey remain within the confines of the economy of salvation, Denis Edwards has pushed the matter further to suggest that even in the order of creation we can discern proper roles of each of the persons (1995; 1999). This is a more direct confrontation with the traditional Western position of the works *ad extra*, and hence of evoking appropriation at all. We shall explore Edwards' position more fully below and simply note at this stage that it marks the end point of a trajectory that finds its origins in Rahner's writings on the Trinity. As I have already noted above, most contemporary theologians view the whole project as yet another dead end inherited from the Western tradition, the sooner ditched the better. My task however is to see what, if anything, might be worth saving from this tradition.

Functions of Meaning and Appropriation[63]

Above I spoke of the doctrine of appropriation being used to stretch the limits of cognitive meaning, while remaining faithful to that meaning. Appropriation allows us to say more than can be said, while being true to the basic elements of the faith. While acknowledging the importance of the cognitive function of meaning we can also ask what other functions meaning might fulfil. To assist in this we draw upon Lonergan's notion of the functions of meaning, these being the cognitive, constitutive, effective and communicative functions.

Firstly, meaning has a communicative function. The meaning grasped by one is communicated to another through gesture, art, symbols, words and through a life well lived. Primarily, Jesus communicates his own Trinitarian life to his disciples through his own prayer (Abba, father), his parables, his intimate sharing of his own Spirit. Jesus talks about his Father in heaven, about the Spirit that fills him, and invites his followers to share in these with him. Secondarily, his disciples continue this process of communication through the gestures, art, symbols, words and life well lived, initiating us all into the life of the Trinity. The written word of the Scriptures plays a major role in this communication of Trinitarian meaning. This communicative function is furthered in the writings of the early Church Fathers, in liturgies, prayers and homilies, as they communicate to their listeners the "truth" of the Trinity in symbolic, artistic modes, by drawing their audience into the very life of the Trinity itself.

Secondly, meaning is constitutive, that is, it constitutes the identity of the Christian community. The language of the Scriptures constitutes the community as a Trinitarian community at its very core. We are members of the body of Christ, Christ lives in us, Christ calls us his friends, we are sons and daughters in the Son; we are temples of the Holy Spirit, the Spirit is poured into our hearts, and prays in the depths of our hearts; we are adopted sons and daughters of the Father and coheirs of the Kingdom, the Son goes to make a home for us in his Father's house. In these ways we can see that the Scriptures convey to the Christian community a sense of its Trinitarian identity.

These constitutive and communicative roles of meaning are continued in the way in which the Trinitarian language of the Scriptures permeates our liturgies, hymns, prayers, art, and so on. This language continues to shape our faith imaginations through the Trinitarian symbolisms and narratives of the Scriptures and the liturgy.

Thirdly, meaning has an effective function. It moves people to action and transforms their living. The Scriptures move us towards a life of action and of mission. We are called to "go and make disciples, in the name of the Father, Son and Spirit" (Mt 28:19). Just as the Father sends the Son, so we too are sent. We are missioned by the Father, to follow in the footsteps of the Son, empowered by his Spirit poured into our hearts. Transformed by the mission of the Son we are called to live in qualitatively different ways, ways which reflect the Trinitarian glory of God.

Finally meaning has a cognitive function, that is, the meaning expressed makes a claim to approximate what really is, the truth, what is real, what is so. The cognitive function of meaning invites us to appropriate the meaning of Scripture as true, while not neglecting the fact that this truth is conveyed through a variety of literary means. As Christians we believe that the Scriptures convey truth, but as intelligent historically conscious believers we appreciate the fact that the truth is not immediate in the text, but is mediated by the mode of expression appropriate to the type of literature used. This precludes the possibility of using Scripture as a source of proof texts, which was largely the approach of the early Church Fathers, as well as the early heretics. On the other hand, to deny or exclude any cognitive function of the meaning of the Scriptures would be to reduce the meaning to being merely metaphorical, without any significant truth claim at all. This is not an uncommon strategy in some theology, for instance in the work of Haight (1999, esp. 8–12), where he makes explicit his commitment to a purely symbolic model of revelation. One can understand the whole movement from the Scriptures to the early Church councils as one of crystallising a precise cognitive meaning from the multiple functions of meaning operative in the New Testament as a whole.

I now propose that attention to the notion of functions of meaning might assist us in reappropriating the doctrine of appropriation in a modern theological context. This may allow us to have a clearer sense of why we might want to say "more than can be said" cognitively while still remaining faithful to that cognitive meaning. The communicative, constitutive and effective functions of meaning are valid functions of meaning, though it might not always be possible to ground these functions in a precise cognitive meaning. For example, my affirmation that my football team is "the best" serves a communicative and effective function of meaning, which remains valid despite defeats the team may suffer from other teams. The range of "appropriate" Trinitarian language can be significantly expanded through forays into these other functions of meaning, faithfully and intelligently moving beyond the bounds of cognitive meaning so as to assist in "manifesting" the truth of our faith.

There remains the question of how this process can be controlled so that the appropriations of non-cognitive functions of meaning are not just arbitrary claims being made without foundation. Augustine and Aquinas used appropriation in two ways. The first was in relation to expressions found in the Scriptures and tradition. This is readily assimilable in terms of the functions of meaning, though our more critical forms of exegesis may make us hesitate to make all the appropriations adopted by these two theologians. The other is by way of analogy, primarily the psychological analogy, which provides a more critical control of meaning in the process of appropriation. We can reappropriate the doctrine of appropriation as a method for extending Trinitarian language beyond the constraints of cognitive meaning, to express communicative, constitutive and effective meaning, a process which we critically control through the deployment of adequate analogies. As we shall see the psychological analogy is just one option available for this process.

Three Examples of Appropriation

In order to explore this suggestion I will analyse the writings of three Trinitarian theologians, Hans Urs von Balthasar, John Zizioulas and Denis Edwards. Each of these theologians has taken Trinitarian theology in striking new directions. Yet I suggest that each "says more than can be said" in a cognitively coherent manner, at least from the perspective of the classical Western tradition. On the other hand it is possible to makes sense of the contribution of each of these theologians from within that tradition through a reappropriation of the notion of appropriation.

Balthasar, communicative meaning and the paschal mystery

Balthasar is a major twentieth century theologian whose writings have a reputation for their density and cultural richness. They are idiosyncratic in that they draw on Balthasar's vast storehouse of cultural knowledge which is largely unmatched and unreproducible. He was a regular critic of Rahner's theological project, which he viewed as too anthropocentric, too congenial to modernity and too complacent in dealing with the demands of the Gospel (Vorgrimler 1986, 124). He described the difference between them in terms of their divergent Enlightenment origins—Rahner followed Kant, while Balthasar followed Goethe, the great German poet (Barron 2000, 7). As a consequence Balthasar is far less concerned with philosophical precision and far more concerned with aesthetic power. Beauty is a key concern: the glory of the Lord which grasps us prior to any intellectualising or moralising. For Balthasar, faith is an aesthetic act, grasping the beauty of the form of divine revelation.

A key question for Balthasar is how we are to understand the immanent Trinity in light of the paschal mystery, the drama of Jesus' death, descent into hell and resurrection. Balthasar reads back into the immanent Trinity many aspects of this drama, finding in the immanent Trinity the ground for the possibility of the economic drama. This is clearly a very different starting point from the rest of the Western tradition with which he makes only tangential contact. Balthasar is critical of most aspects of the Western tradition, particularly the psychological analogy, but also traditional notions of impassibility and immutability.[64] It is difficult to establish an effective dialogue between Balthasar and the Western tradition because his whole methodology is so unique, his style so personal, and his language so poetic. Nonetheless this does not negate the necessity of critical thinking in relation to his thought.

The starting point for this discussion of his theology is his understanding of the persons of the Trinity and the way in which their relationships ground the possibility of creation. He views the Trinitarian processions in terms of the categories of "separation and union": "That God (as Father) can so give away his divinity that God (as Son), does not merely receive it as something borrowed, but possesses it in the equality of essence, expresses such an unimaginable and unsurpassable 'separation' of God from Godself that every other separation (made possible by it!), even the most dark and bitter, can only occur within the first 'separation'" (Hunt 1997, 60). Balthasar speaks of this separation as an "eternal super-Kenosis" by which the Father "makes himself 'destitute' of all that he is and can be so as to bring forth a consubstantial divinity, the Son" (ibid). The "separation" between Father and Son creates the "space" for all the contingencies of human freedom, so that the drama of the world becomes a "play within the play" of the larger divine drama. "We are saying that the 'emptying' of the Father's heart in the begetting of the Son includes and surpasses every possible drama between God and the world, because a world can only have its place within the difference between the Father and the Son which is held open and bridged over by the Spirit" (ibid). As an example of the cross-over between the immanent and economic Trinity Balthasar seeks to express links between the immanent and economic experiences of the Son and Father and Spirit. Thus the Son's experience of opposition in the God-forsakenness of death and descent are a function or modality of the Son's loving relationship to the Father and Spirit. The economic drama is grounded in an immanent drama of the self-yielding surrender of divine being.

One difficulty here is the way in which it seems to place the immanent Trinity within a framework of events and change. While Balthasar rejects any univocal attribution of change in God, as in process thought, he also rejects as inadequate talk of divine immutability or impassibility. Similarly, he rejects temporality but speaks of "supra-temporality." Nonetheless, he wants to posit a real kenosis in God, a real self-emptying, as an "event" in God that has ontological and not merely functional or soteriological status.

From this dramatic starting point Balthasar seeks to present a Trinitarian account of the paschal mystery, the death, descent and resurrection of Jesus. A number of modern authors have attempted similar accounts in relation to the death and resurrection but Balthasar is alone in dealing with the "descent into hell" in a Trinitarian manner.[65]

Beginning with the crucifixion, Balthasar views Jesus' death as an event of self-surrender, even abandonment. Jesus dies "God-forsaken," with reference to Jesus' cry from the cross. Still this abandonment remains a modality of the inner-Trinitarian event; indeed it is the "highest worldly revelation" of the event of difference between Father and Son in the Spirit. Similarly, the obedience of the Son reflects the Son's inner-Trinitarian love for the Father.

One significant feature of Balthasar's theology is his redefinition of the notion of person in terms of mission, rather than a being with a rational nature, or a conscious subject. It is only in the address of God which "shows him the purpose of his existence," that is, imparts a mission, that the conscious subject becomes a "person." In this sense Balthasar maintains a perfect identity between the person of Jesus as Son and his mission: "The point of identity is his mission from God (*missio*), which is identical with the Person *in* God and *as* God (*processio*)" (Hunt 1997, 67). Here it would be very easy to read this as saying that without the mission of Jesus there would be no second person of the Trinity, or that the Jesus is only a divine person when he receives his mission at, for example, the baptism (which would constitute an adoptionist position).

Undoubtedly the most imaginative and certainly unique contribution that Balthasar makes is in relation to the theme of the descent into hell as part of the paschal mystery. This relatively minor part of the biblical (1 Pt 3:18–20) and creedal tradition (a mention in the Apostle's Creed) becomes, in the hands of Balthasar, a major part of the redemptive work of Jesus, and as always reflective of an inner-Trinitarian drama. Hunt identifies five key elements in his treatment of the descent:

(i) far form being active, the descent is instead an utterly passive "sinking down." It reveals Jesus' solidarity in human death.

(ii) the descent also represents Jesus' solidarity with humanity in its sinfulness. In the descent his solidarity extends to those who are dead in a theological sense. In the utter defencelessness of love he enters into the loneliness and desolation of the sinner.

(iii) in accompanying the sinner in hell God freely and lovingly shares in the exercise of human freedom. The reality of human freedom is thus affirmed, including the dramatic possibility of rejecting God. Here Balthasar addresses the relationship between divine and created freedom.

(iv) in the descent Jesus suffers what Balthasar refers to as a "second death" in which Jesus sees "sin in itself." The reality of sin is acknowledged, but in the context of the ever greater love of God.

(v) the descent is a Trinitarian event. At this point Balthasar strains to the ultimate paradox: that in the descent, in this loss of glory, the glory of the Lord is revealed. (1997, 68–69)

The overall effect of this account of the descent is a powerful affirmation of the universal salvific will of God, which for Balthasar is manifest even in God's willing to enter into "hell," to offer the sinner a final act of solidarity, of saving love. He respects the reality of human freedom, but also asserts the divine sovereignty so that God's freedom is not thwarted by that human freedom. God's freedom does not coerce the sinner, but transforms the sinner from the inside by "freely entering into our lostness and our hellish desolation." For Balthasar, even hell is a "sphere" within God.

For Balthasar the descent is only possible because God is triune—the Father sends the Son into hell. The Son, while remaining God, descends into Godforsakeness, accompanying the sinner in their choice to damn themselves. The Spirit accompanies the Son as the bond between Father and Son, uniting them in their separation. Indeed this bond "is stretched to breaking point." Further, the obedience of the Son displayed in the descent is a modality of his love for the Father. He enters into the depths of sinful existence and separation from God: "Thereby, … the eternal will of the Son within the Trinity to obedience is exposed, as the substructure that is the basis of the entire event of the Incarnation: and this is set face-to-face with the hidden substructure of sinful existence, exposed in Sheol, as the state of separation from God, the 'loss of glory'" (ibid. 75–76). Turning to the resurrection Balthasar views it as a further sign of the obedience of the Son who allows the Father to raise him from the dead. The Father now shows the world his risen Son, now become what as God he always was. The Spirit is also involved as the "instrument" or "milieu" of the resurrection. The reunion of the Father and Son is then the condition of the breathing forth of the Spirit into the world as from a single principle. In this way, the resurrection shows that the Spirit proceeds from the Father and the Son, as the expression of their united freedom.

In all this we can understand Balthasar as attempting to draw an analogy between the paschal mystery and the immanent Trinity: "God is in the paschal mystery what God is eternally," a variant and specification of Rahner's *grundaxiom* (ibid. 84). Further to this, Balthasar presents the inner-Trinitarian relationships as modelled on inter-personal relationships. In fact, as I have suggested, inter-personal human relationships may not be a good way to model the inner-Trinitarian relationships, precisely because one set of relations are necessary and natural, the others are contingent and free. I shall comment further on this in the section on the work of John Zizioulas below.

In some ways the use of interpersonal categories might be a consequence of the misuse of Rahner's axiom and its variants. In the economic Trinity the person of the Son engages a human will, which is distinct from that of the will of the Father (which is the divine will, and also the divine will of the Son and the Spirit). To speak of the freedom of the Son, and of the will of the Son is thus an ambiguous statement, one which tends to blur the distinction between the human and divine natures of the Son. Balthasar plays with this blurring in a way which attempts to bring interpersonal categories into the immanent Trinity, as when he speaks of the "eternal will of the Son within the Trinity" as obedient to the will of the Father. Balthasar blurs the dogmatic distinction between person and nature as and when it suits him.

As with his account of creation, Balthasar's account of the paschal mystery as a Trinitarian event draws on dramatic and poetic language, but it is difficult to see where much of it can be grounded, or what evidence there is apart from his own assertions. The theme of the descent is a case in point. Balthasar speaks powerfully of the love of God for the sinner, reaching even into the depths of hell. But its basis in the tradition, as a matter of fact, is very slim and its strict justification most difficult. Balthasar has created a moving account but the categories are largely those of the imagination, of space and time. Without great care this type of writing can spin out of control, and transform belief in the Trinity into an elaborate religious myth.

Perhaps the most constructive way to consider this material is under the category of communicative meaning, that is a process of communication through the gestures, art, symbols, words and life well lived, initiating us all into the life of the Trinity through the events of the paschal mystery.[66] Just as the Scriptures present us with a dramatic Trinitarian narrative of the events of salvation, Balthasar is filling in the gaps in the narrative, in the light of the more developed Trinitarian and Christological doctrines of the Church. Balthasar describes his work as a theological aesthetic. The criteria he wants us to judge his work by are aesthetic, though they remain primarily theological. He views his work as a theological aesthetic, not an aesthetical theology (Balthasar 1983, 79–127). Still at the level of cognitive meaning there have to be big question marks over his approach. As Hunt notes, "the question remains whether von Balthasar is finally coherent" (1997, 85). Whatever level of control there is in this process is achieved through the creative analogy drawn between the immanent Trinity and the economic Trinity revealed in the paschal mystery.

Zizioulas, constitutive meaning and the mystery of the Church

Few ecclesiological topics have been embraced with as much enthusiasm as the notion that the Church is a communion—*communio* or *koinonia*—which reflects the communion of the Trinity itself. The Vatican II dogmatic constitution on the Church, *Lumen Gentium* states it thus: "the universal Church is seen to be 'a people brought into unity from the unity of the Father, the Son and the Holy Spirit'" (LG n.4). This notion of the Church as reflecting the communion/*koinonia*/*perichoresis* of the Trinity can be found in a large number of theological writings, in particular those of John Zizioulas. Zizioulas is a major theologian in the Eastern Orthodox tradition and his writings have been significant in bringing the insights of that tradition to light in the West. They have influenced a number of theologians, both in the Reformed and the Catholic tradition.

Zizioulas raises the basic questions of the relationship between the Trinitarian God and the Church in the following manner: "If the very being of God in whom we believe is *koinonia*, and if the person of Christ in whose name we human beings and the whole of creation are saved is also in his very being *koinonia*, what consequences does this faith entail for our understanding of the Church? How does the notion of *koinonia* affect the Church's identity, her structure and her ministry in the world? ... Finally, how can the understanding of Church as *koinonia* affect her mission in the world, including her relation with the entire creation?" (Zizioulas 1994, 6–7). This is echoed by Walter Kasper who notes, "the communion of the Church is prefigured, made possible and sustained by the communion of the Trinity ... it is precisely as communion that the church is an icon of the Trinity" (1989, 152).

Much of the argument for these positions is based on the insight from Trinitarian theology that the notion of person is relational. In the Trinity we find that the persons are defined by their relationships, that is, the Father is who he is because of his relationship with the Son and Spirit, the Son because of his relationship with Father and Spirit, and the Spirit because of his relationship with Father and Son. This relational conception of persons can be used to argue against modern conceptions of individualism. Human persons too are relational, not isolated individuals. It is only in the *communio* of the Church itself that we fully realise our relational potential and so fully become persons. To quote Zizioulas: "Love is a relationship, it is the free coming out of oneself ... it is the other and our relationship with him that gives us our identity, our otherness, making us "who we are" i.e. persons; for by being an inseparable part of a relationship that matters ontologically we emerge as unique and irreplaceable entities. This therefore is what accounts for our being, and being ourselves and not someone else—our personhood" (1985, 88). So the questions we must face are how helpful these Trinitarian considerations are in our understanding of human persons and of the Church. Do the inner-Trinitarian relations tell us anything about our own situation?

Certainly one of the key insights of Trinitarian theology, both Eastern and Western, is that the divine persons are constituted by their mutual relations; indeed a Thomistic analysis would argue that the persons are subsistent relations, that is, their relationality is their personal identity. Thus the Father is his paternity, and so on for the other persons. Still there are many different types of relationships and not all relationships are appropriate in dealing with the persons of the Trinity. What is in fact a very minimal notion in the Western tradition, little more than a directed arrow (a relationship of origin), has taken on modern connotations of interpersonal relationship, with all that might imply.

Consider some examples of human relationships: (i) I am shorter than my son; (ii) I am the father of my son; (iii) I love my son. The first is true, but is hardly a personal relationship. It is accidental and says nothing about our personal identities. The second is also true, and it is in some sense constitutive of both our identities as father and son. It remains true whether I am a good or bad father, he a good or bad son. We cannot change it; it may or may not have been the result of an original free decision, but once established it is no longer subject to either of our free decisions. The third is more fully personal and expresses a quality of our (pre-existing) relationship. It is an essentially free and personal relationship. But it is not necessarily constitutive of our identities as father and son. If it were I would cease to be father and he my son if I ceased to love him.

How then do we conceive of the relationship between the Father and the Son? Which of the alternatives, for example, best relates to the relationship between the Father and the Son? Zizioulas clearly conceives of the relationship along the lines of the third possibility. As Fox states of Zizioulas' position, "The Father as a person freely wills communion with the Spirit and the Son" (2001, 40). Freedom is constitutive of personhood for Zizioulas, and hence must be constitutive of the inner-Trinitarian relationship.

From within the Western tradition the problem with this is fairly clear. What can be freely willed, or is the product of decision, is contingent upon that decision. But God is necessary being, in whom nothing is contingent. The contingent relates to the order of creation. In the case of a contingent relationship, either the Son and Spirit would be creatures and hence not divine; or the Son and Spirit have distinct freedoms, in violation of the *homoousios*. The conclusion of the Western tradition is that the Father does not "will" his relationship with the Son, nor with the Spirit. Its conception of the Father-Son relationship is closer to the second of the three above.

Aquinas considers this question in ST I q41 a2: "Whether the notional acts are voluntary?," that is, are the acts which belong specifically to the persons (notional acts), such as the Father speaking the Word, or the Father and Son spirating the Spirit, free acts. He responds:

> When anything is said to be, or to be made by the will, this can be understood in two senses. In one sense, the ablative designates only concomitance, as I can say that I am a man by my will—that is, I will to be a man; and in this way it can be said that the Father begot the Son by will; as also He is God by will, because He wills to be God, and wills to beget the Son. In the other sense, the ablative imports the habitude of a principle as it is said that the workman works by his will, as the will is the principle of his work; and thus in that sense it must be said the God the Father begot the Son, not by His will; but that He produced the creature by His will. ... Wherefore Hilary says (*De Synod.*): "The will of God gave to all creatures their substance: but perfect birth gave the Son a nature derived from a substance impassible and unborn. All things created are such as God willed them to be; but the Son, born of God, subsists in the perfect likeness of God."

The first of these two senses is very broad. It denotes the "willing acceptance" of my own reality. As such it is not "free" in the usual sense, but in some sense necessary, but again not in the sense of being pre-personal or mechanistic. Here the psychological analogy shows it strength. In terms of the psychological analogy we find a way of understanding the processions of the Son and Spirit as "personal" without them being "deliberate," that is, "willed" in a sense that would make them creatures. Aquinas describes the processions in terms of "intelligible emanations," emanations which are "because," a personal form of causation which is not willed, but is necessary in a personal sense, a rational necessity not a mechanistic necessity. Without this type of analysis Zizioulas' suggestion that the Father wills his communion with the Son and Spirit can easily lead to problems of subordinationism or tritheism.

In this sense then it is quite misleading to describe the relationship of the Father to the Son as one of love, if we are talking of the relationship that mutually constitutes each as persons. Aquinas would say the Father loves the Son with the same love with which he loves himself and the Spirit (and all creation!), that is, through an essential act of the divine nature. For there is one will in God and hence one love—see for instance his handling of the Augustinian notion that the Spirit is the mutual love of the Father and Son (ST I q37 a2). Lest this emphasis on the oneness of the divine will seem a purely Western preoccupation, we can note the position of Vladimir Lossky, who states: "The divine attributes relate to common nature: intelligence, will, love, peace concern the three hypostases together and cannot differentiate them" (1978, 43).

This raises questions as to whether the relationships within the Trinity are a right and proper model for our relationships within the Church. Relationships within the Church are the product of a freely entered, faith relationship. Any *communio* or fellowship within the Church is intimate and personal only inasmuch as, and precisely because, it is freely enter into by its participants. It is not coerced nor is it "natural" as in a family relationship. On the other hand the intimacy or *perichoresis* of the divine persons is what it is precisely because and inasmuch as it is not freely entered into, but is natural, though still personal. This highlights the limitations of using the analogy of the *perichoresis* of the persons of the Trinity as a basis for understanding the nature of the Church.

This is perhaps an instance of where constitutive meaning might outstrip what can be said cognitively. While we share in the divine intimacy through the life of grace, our ecclesial relationship with one another can only be analogously likened to the Trinitarian relationships. At the level of constitutive meaning such an analogy may be a powerful symbol of Christian ecclesial identity and self-understanding. However, we must also be aware of the limitations of the analogy, as noted above. Without such an awareness it would be easy to draw conclusions, such as tritheism, which are counter to the faith of both Eastern and Western traditions.

Edwards, effective meaning and the psychological analogy

The writings of Denis Edwards take us in yet another direction in Trinitarian theology. In his various writings Edwards (1995; 1999) has attempted to extend traditional Western understandings of the Trinity by bringing them into dialogue with contemporary biblical and scientific studies. Two major elements in this are the recovery of the Wisdom/Sophia biblical tradition as an alternative form of expression to the Logos Christology that has dominated the Western tradition (here Edwards is drawing on the writings of Elizabeth Johnson and others); and the incorporation of an evolutionary understanding of the cosmos and its congruence with Trinitarian understandings of persons in relationship. In this way Edwards, like Balthasar, Moltmann and process theologians, questions traditional understandings of divine immutability to allow for creation to have a real effect on the divine being. In some sense then, God suffers the pangs of creation and the affront of human sinfulness.

This debate draws upon and reacts against an element of the Western tradition that speaks of the relationship between God and creatures as "real" on the part of creatures and "logical" on the part of God. The relationship between the creature and God is "real" on the side of the creature because it is constitutive of the being of the creature. The creature would not be what it is, or even exist, without this relationship. On the other hand, because of divine transcendence, God's being is not constituted by the relationship with the creature.

God would still be God without it. While the language of real versus logical relations is meant to preserve divine transcendence, it also leads to the impression that God does not care ("is really relating to") creation. Theologians who wish to speak of God as really related to creation imply that creation impacts upon God and so God is really responsive to creation. In this sense then God suffers, because of the impact of an unpredictable creation, including the effect of human sinfulness (1995, 122–30; 1999, 35–55).

Edwards then seeks to develop this notion of a real relationship between God and creation into a Trinitarian frame. He suggests that not only should we view God as really related to creation, but we should also view the persons of the Trinity as related to creation in distinctive ways: "Creation is the action of the whole Trinity, but it needs to be seen as involving the distinct roles of the Trinitarian Persons, which are not only 'appropriated' to them, but 'proper' to them" (1995, 118). In particular Edwards wants to argue that "the Spirit of God can be understood as the immanent presence of God in all things … this Holy Spirit … is that which connects all created things in God." The Logos, on the other hand, is "the one in whom all things were created," the "divine Image and Exemplar" (ibid. 119–21). Clearly Edwards understands his position as moving beyond the strictures of the classical doctrine of appropriations.

Part of the motivation for seeking to move beyond the traditional doctrine of appropriation can be found in Edwards' interest in the current ecological debate. Edwards views the interconnectedness of the created biosphere as reflecting the interrelatedness of the divine persons of the Trinity. Creation reflects the divine glory precisely as Trinitarian: "This means that the rain forest of the Amazon is to be understood as the self-expression of the divine Trinity. It is a sacrament of God's presence. Its vitality and exuberance spring from the immanent presence of the Spirit, the giver of life. They express the Trinitarian love of life. The rain forest, in its form, function and beauty as a harmonious biotic community is the work of art of divine Wisdom. The species of plants and animals which are being destroyed forever are modes of God's self-communication and presence" (ibid. 117). It is clear that Edwards wants us to understand this in light of his later arguments for proper roles for the Spirit and Word in creation

(1995, 118–22). It is also clear what problems arise from the perspective of the Western tradition. This tradition has always baulked at any suggestion that would compromise the divine transcendence, and so would not accept the notion of a real relation between God and the creature. However it does recognise distinctive roles in the economy of salvation for the distinct persons. For example, only the Logos is incarnate in human history. Is there an objection to extending these distinctive roles into the created order precisely as created? In fact one can envisage two immediate objections.

The first is that the attempt to introduce proper roles for the Trinitarian persons in the created order blurs the distinction between the natural and supernatural orders. At its simplest the distinction between these two orders can be understood in terms of whether a reality relates to divinity *per se* (natural order) or to the persons in some distinct fashion (supernatural). The attempt to introduce proper roles in the order of creation can be read as an attempt to supernaturalise the natural order.[67] While a number of theologians have moved in this direction, it creates problems in dealing with the question of sin. Either sin breaks our supernatural relationship with God or it does not. If it does, given we supernaturalise the natural, we can only conclude that in sinning we cease to be, because our creaturely relationship is already supernatural. This is clearly not the case. On the other hand, if it does not break our supernatural relationship, sin loses its seriousness. It is precisely in order to resolve this difficulty that scholastic theology introduced the natural order into its theology of grace, and so allowed for two distinct types of relationships between God and the creature (three if one includes the incarnation). Hence Aquinas speaks of three forms of divine presence: by essence, presence and power, by which the Creator is naturally present to all creatures; by sanctifying grace, by which God dwells in holy men and women; and by personal union which is proper to the incarnation (ST III q2 a19 ad2). In this way Aquinas was able to overcome problems he had inherited from Augustine in the area of sin and grace.

The second difficulty is related to the first, but in the area of revelation. If the persons of the Trinity have distinctive roles in the created order, then one could argue that they can be known as distinct, simply from that order. The distinct effects of the distinct roles of each person would lead one to conclude to distinct persons (Of course this argument loses its force if one holds that it is not possible to know the existence of God through natural means. If such a natural theology is not possible, then clearly one could not deduce a Trinitarian God either. However, if one holds with the Western tradition that natural knowledge of God is possible, then Edwards' position causes problems). The Trinity would then be naturally knowable. As such this project is an extension of earlier arguments of a more rationalist bent that sought to find the Trinity by an examination of divine attributes.

It is of interest to see how Aquinas handles this same type of question in ST I q34 a3:

> Whether the name "Word" imports relation to creatures? ...
> OBJ 1: It would seem that the name "Word" does not import relation to creatures. For every name that connotes some effect in creatures, is said of God essentially. But Word is not said essentially, but personally. Therefore Word does not import relation to creatures...
>
> I answer that, Word implies relation to creatures. For God by knowing Himself, knows every creature. Now the word conceived in the mind is representative of everything that is actually understood. Hence there are in ourselves different words for the different things which we understand. But because God by one act understands Himself and all things, His one only Word is expressive not only of the Father, but of all creatures.
>
> And as the knowledge of God is only cognitive as regards God, whereas as regards creatures, it is both cognitive and operative, so the Word of God is only expressive of what is in God the Father, but is both expressive and operative of creatures; ...
>
> Reply OBJ 1: The nature is also included indirectly in the name of the person; for person is an individual substance of a rational nature. Therefore the name of a divine person, as regards the personal relation, does not imply relation to the creature, but it is implied in what belongs to the nature. Yet there is nothing to prevent its implying relation to creatures, so far as the essence is included in its meaning: for as it properly belongs to the Son to be the Son, so it properly belongs to Him to be God begotten, or the Creator begotten; and in this way the name Word imports relation to creatures.

We can see here both affirmation and negation—yes there is a relation, but it is an implied relation "in what belongs to the [divine] nature," which is of course common to all three persons. This is precisely the role for appropriation, to say what cannot be said in a more direct cognitive sense.

It is here perhaps helpful to distinguish between the cognitive and effective functions of meaning. Edwards' argument can be read as employing an effective function of meaning, which may motivate a Christian community to greater ecological concern. This is a valid and valuable project in light of criticism levelled at Christians for their neglect of environmental concerns.[68] However, this effective role is also self-limiting. The effective function of meaning is "effective" within a Christian community because it elicits Trinitarian faith, but not effective beyond it. In fact beyond it, the evocation of such an explicitly Christian meaning may in fact be alienating. Ecological concern is not restricted to Christians, but is a common human concern, which should stand on a more common ethical ground. This is to raise a more difficult and much debated issue as to the relationship between Christian and other ethics. Without entering into this debate, it is clear that the way in which Edwards views the proper roles of the persons might well imply that only a specifically and explicitly Christian ethics is valid.

Finally we should note that the controlling analogy here is basically the psychological analogy. Though Edwards prefers the more neo-Platonic theology of Bonaventure, who speaks of the Father as "Fountain Fullness," the Son as "Divine Image and Exemplar" and the Spirit as "Bond of Love," he also acknowledges a similar formulation in Aquinas, which he quotes (ST I q45 a7). Aquinas' argument here is based on the psychological analogy, as it is in ST I q34 a3 above. The psychological analogy provides a framework for identifying appropriated roles for the Father as creator, the Son as meaning, form or image of creation and the Spirit as ecstatic value of creation.

Conclusion

The question which we have sought to address is whether the traditional Western doctrine of appropriation still has a role in a contemporary theology of the Trinity. I have suggested that it may be possible to reframe this doctrine in terms of what Lonergan calls "functions of meaning." The problem we face is whether we must restrict our theological discourse to what can be cognitively affirmed as true, or whether we allow broader functions of meaning to be part of that discourse. Aquinas acknowledged this broader form of discourse as appropriate "for the *manifestation* of our faith" (ST I q39 a7). However, if we do not allow for this broader discourse we shall either mistake our communicative, constitutive and effective meanings as already cognitive; or we greatly impoverish our Trinitarian discourse by restricting it to what can safely be cognitively asserted, which in fact is very little. This approach using the functions of meaning thus helps provide a basic motivation, which was lacking in the classical doctrine of appropriations, for extending our Trinitarian discourse.

Again, as with the classical doctrine of appropriations, the basic control that operates in this process of meaning is that of analogy. The authors we have considered above can be understood as working with three different analogies, that between the immanent Trinity and the Trinity revealed in the paschal mystery (Balthasar), between the Trinity and the Church (Zizioulas) and the psychological analogy (Edwards). Each of these analogies breaks down in some fashion, precisely because they are analogies, not identities. If however we forget the limits of the analogy we may be tempted to think that we are speaking in a cognitive mode rather than in another more "appropriate" function of meaning.

Chapter 6
Wrestling with Rahner on the Trinity[69]

It is commonly held that Karl Rahner has done more than any other Catholic theologian to revitalise the theology of the Trinity in the twentieth century. The general post-Rahnerian verdict would state that Trinitarian theology had been marginalised and reduced to esoteric metaphysical subtleties, thus rendering it irrelevant both to theology and Christian living. The villain in the story is Aquinas with his subtle metaphysics and his reliance on the psychological analogy, at least as it has been mediated by his neo-scholastic interpreters. As a consequence, Rahner argued, most Catholics were little more than "mere" monotheists, with no Trinitarian depth to their spiritual lives. Rahner's aim then was to bring Trinitarian doctrine and theology back into the centre of Christian theology, in particular bringing it into direct contact with Christology and the theology of grace. Though Rahner's major contribution to this process, his book *The Trinity*, was relatively slight, a mere one hundred and twenty pages, and more programmatic than comprehensive, it is clear that his stance has had a significant impact upon all subsequent Trinitarian thought. In particular Rahner's *grundaxiom* on the identity of the economic and immanent Trinity has almost become a theological commonplace, either explicitly or implicitly in the work of most major authors in the area. Certainly none can afford to ignore it.

Still, Rahner has his critics, from neo-scholastics (Mansini 1988), from neo-Barthians (Molnar 1985) and others. We can note the criticism by Balthasar, cited by Vorgrimler, that "Rahner has been the great theological opponent who makes faith inadmissibly easy, who adapts to the needs of contemporaries, and trivializes the seriousness of God's history with humanity" (1986, 124). Johann Baptist Metz (1980, esp. 154ff.) has also been critical of Rahner, particularly his dependence on the transcendental-idealist turn to the subject of German philosophy, embodied in the philosophies of Hegel and Kant. A recent article by Nancy Dallavalle, "Revisiting Rahner: On the theological status of trinitarian theology" has produced a scathing criticism of Rahner's theological project, with a particular focus on Rahner's *grundaxiom*. She concludes that, "left with Rahner, Trinitarian theology could easily end up as impoverished as he saw it to be in the manuals of neo-scholasticism" (Dallavalle 1998, 150). In strong language she speaks of Rahner's axiom leading to the "concomitant evisceration of trinitarian theology," in particular the collapse of the immanent Trinity into the economic Trinity, a concern which some would find validated in various contemporary approaches, such as the work of Catherine LaCugna (1993).

Dallavalle presents a solid case for her position, though it may well be that Rahner himself would not be happy with the trajectory taken by many contemporary theologians who have sought to extend and popularise his basic Trinitarian approach. In this chapter I take Dallavalle's argument further by highlighting other aspects of Rahner's Trinitarian theology which in a similar fashion have led to trajectories within contemporary thought that stand in considerable tension with more traditional Western stances on the Trinity. I will specify two. Firstly, there has been a blurring of the distinction between the categories of person and nature and the subsequent use of intersubjective categories to describe the relationships of the persons in the Trinity. Secondly, Rahner's handling, or rather, non-handling of the *filioque* issue has become, I believe, a problem. A deeper problem is Rahner's theological method and the difficulties it has caused him and the authors who have followed in his footsteps. In this context I shall focus on the Trinitarian theology of David Coffey, with minor references to other authors.

Blurring the Distinction between Person and Nature

In his substantiation of his *grundaxiom*, that "the economic Trinity is the immanent Trinity and vice versa," Rahner spends most of his discussion on the case of the Incarnation of the Logos. He begins with a rejection of the standard scholastic position that any of the three persons of the Trinity could have been incarnated. If this is the case, Rahner argues, "that which God is for us would tell us absolutely nothing about that which he is in himself, as triune" (1974, 30). Further the reality of the incarnation would convey "nothing about the Logos as such ... the human as such would not show us the Logos as such ...when we glimpse the humanity of Christ as such we would in reality see nothing of the subject of the Logos himself, except at most his abstract formal subjectivity" (ibid. 31–32). Instead, he argues, it is because of God's free decision of self-communication that "that precisely is born which we call human nature ... man is possible because the exteriorization of the Logos is possible" (ibid. 33). Rahner concludes, "what Jesus is and does as man reveals the Logos himself; it is the reality of the Logos as our salvation amidst us. Then we can assert, in the full meaning of the words: here the Logos with God and the Logos with us, the immanent and the economic Logos, are strictly the same" (ibid.). Before considering the consequences of such an identification, let me comment on the theological method involved. Rahner rejects the traditional scholastic position, found in Aquinas (ST III q3 a5), that any of the three persons could have been incarnated in a human nature. Aquinas' argument is based on the commonality of the divine power which is the principle of the act of incarnation. As common, it applies equally to all three persons. Nonetheless, Aquinas goes on to argue that it is most fitting that the Son be incarnate, rather than the Father or the Spirit (ST III q3 a8). In other words, while Aquinas pulls back from necessity, he finds the incarnation of the Logos most fitting, most intelligible. Rahner, on the other hand, is not satisfied with such intelligibility, but demands necessity. This distinction between intelligibility and necessity signals quite different conceptions of the theological project, and has implications beyond this present instance.

Let us focus now on his assertion of the strict identity of the immanent and economic Logos. How are we to understand this? A traditional Chalcedonian Christology would assert the identity of the person in this case, namely the person of the immanent Logos is the person of the human being Jesus Christ, the "economic Logos," the Word made flesh (Jn 1:14). However, it would also distinguish between the divine and human natures of the Logos. Hence the "strict identity" is hypostatic, that is, in the realm of the person, but not formal or natural. Indeed any such formal or natural union is excluded by Chalcedon's use of the terms "unmixed and unconfused." Yet it would seem that it is precisely here that Rahner wants to say more. The human nature of Jesus, as such, tells us something about the Logos: "what Jesus is and does as man reveals the Logos himself." "What Jesus is" is a human being, a concrete instance of a human nature. Is this concrete human nature meant to reveal something of the person or of the nature of the Logos? Here Rahner's somewhat confusing category of quasi-formal causality is an essential part of his argument. It further blurs the distinction between the divine person and the divine nature, and the relationship of each to the concrete human being Jesus Christ, who remains nonetheless God-with-us. By speaking of the incarnation in terms of a formal cause, however "quasi," the focus shifts from the personal or hypostatic character of the union, to a formal or natural union, something on the level of the natures involved.

The first and most obvious consequence of this blurring is this: it fails to maintain speculatively the dogmatic distinction found in Chalcedon between the categories of person and nature.[70] The result, inevitably, is either a Monophysite or Nestorian Christology. Some conservative critics have indeed claimed Rahner's Christology is Nestorian (Siri 1975). A more balanced but critical appraisal is presented by Raymond Moloney (1999). Moloney notes that Rahner's account of Jesus' immediate vision of God as Jesus' human soul knowing the Word, "raised the spectre of a Nestorian duality of subjects" (ibid. 128). But a case could equally be made that it is Monophysite. In the writings of David Coffey, who remains a faithful though critical student of Rahner and his method, we find this speculative difficulty worked out to its logical conclusions. Coffey has indeed conceded that his recent stance could be conceived as "monophysitism from below" (1999, 412). On the other hand Paul Molnar has argued that Coffey's position is adoptionist, with all its Nestorian overtones (2002).[71] I suggest that what we have here is a speculative failure to distinguish between the categories of person and nature. This speculative confusion is present in Rahner's work and has been adopted by Coffey. The unfortunate result has been a fundamental instability in the Christological position of both.

Let us look more closely at Coffey's position in this regard. In his paper, "The 'Incarnation' of the Holy Spirit in Christ" (1984), Coffey understands Rahner's Christology to be based on the insight that "the divinity of Christ is not something different from his humanity; it *is* the humanity, i.e., human nature at the peak of its possibility, which is the achievement of God's grace" (ibid. 467). What saves this position from being Monophysite, in Coffey's view, is that "the divine person is not given *absolutely* perfect expression in the human nature of Christ, but only the perfection of expression *relative* to the capacity of human nature" (ibid. 468). Furthermore, Coffey acknowledges this insight as fundamental to his own work on Spirit Christology. What has held back this insight is, in his own terms, "the belief that the divinity of Christ was ontologically different from his humanity" (ibid. 469). This same position is repeated in his later writings (1986, 239; 1999b 412–14).

Clearly a blurring of the distinction between person and nature is in evidence. What exactly, then, is being asserted when it is stated that the divinity of Christ is not something different from his humanity? What is implied when it is stated that the divinity of Christ is not ontologically different from his humanity? If the divinity refers to the divine nature, then clearly there is a significant ontological difference. If it refers to the divine person of the Logos, then we find confusion between the categories of person and nature at work. To be fair, Coffey seems aware of the problem and seeks to address it in a later article on the topic. To quote at length:

> The thesis that Christ's human nature is theandric becomes inevitable once human nature is defined in terms of orientation to God. Though also divine, Christ's human nature remains basically and integrally human, and therefore, to put it negatively, incapable of states of being or operation that are strictly divine … But if this nature is also in a sense divine, it remains a nature and does not itself become the person of the Word; it merely becomes a nature possible and suitable for assumption by the Word. While is it true (and important) to stress that the Word assumed a human nature like ours, it is also true that it is rendered unique, theandric, in the act of assumption. (Coffey 1999b, 412–13)

Significantly Coffey thinks that this clarification addresses concerns previously raised by McDermott that Rahner "confused nature and person" (ibid. 412 n.23). Yet it is difficult to see how this basic problem is being addressed. If anything it confirms the concern that a basic confusion exists. Take for example the statement, "though also divine,

Christ's human nature remains basically and integrally human." To what does the word "divine" refer—person or nature? If nature, then it seems to assert that Christ's human nature is divine by sharing somehow in the divine nature. This verges on the Monophysite. On the other hand, if it refers to the divine person, then there is a blurring of the distinction between (the divine) *person* and (the human) *nature*. One could ask the same questions about the assertion, "if this nature is also in a sense divine, it remains a nature and does not itself become the person of the Word." Chalcedon does not assert that the human nature of Jesus is divine in any sense, but that the human being Jesus Christ is a divine person.

A second consequence of this confusion is the covert justification for the introduction of a certain kind of interpersonal categories into the Trinitarian relationships. This may seem an odd objection to make. Given the large-scale adoption of such categories in modern Trinitarian theology, an interpersonal consideration of the Trinitarian life is being hailed as a major advance in theological thought. But there is a problem concealed here. Let me explain further.

Consider again Rahner's identification of the immanent and economic Logos. Now there are many things we can say about the economic Logos, the incarnate Word, Jesus Christ in terms of his relationship to the Father. He is obedient to the will of the Father, he loves the Father, he prays to the Father. We may rightly deploy a whole series of interpersonal categories to describe this relationship. Nonetheless, in classical terms the validity of these interpersonal statements depends upon their application to the incarnate human being, Jesus of Nazareth. For example we may speak of the love of Jesus for the Father in terms of an act of the human will of Jesus, and similarly with respect to obedience. However, it is less clear that these same categories can be used of the immanent relationship between Father and Son in the Trinity. In what sense, if any, is the immanent Logos obedient to the Father? (This question can certainly be addressed to the Trinitarian theology of Balthasar, as noted in the previous chapter.) Within the divinity, the *homoousios* implies a single divine will, equally that of the Father, Son and Spirit. Unless one were to fall into a Monothelite Christology, the divine will of the immanent Logos is distinct from the human will of the economic incarnate Logos. In this case one cannot read back from the economic Trinity truths about the immanent Trinity. In this sense at least the immanent Logos is not strictly the same as the economic Logos. There is no clear reason why inter-personal realities grounded in the human will of Jesus can or should be read back into statements about the immanent Logos. More summarily Lonergan observes, "The person of the Word can speak and actually does speak in accordance with his human nature. But in his divine nature the person of the Word neither can nor does speak but is only spoken" (2002, 225).

The problem is amplified in the works of Coffey who seeks to develop the Augustinian notion of the Spirit as the mutual love of the Father and Son. The status of this in Augustine's own theological corpus remains problematic. To my mind, it is just one of a number of explorations and experiments that Augustine conducts in *De Trinitate*; and is not his most successful. The full extent of the difficulties associated with Augustine on this point is evidenced in Aquinas' rather strained reading of Augustine's position, such that he transforms, indeed deconstructs, it into a variation of the *filioque* (ST I q37 a2). Aquinas recognises that there is only one essential love, shared by Father, Son and Spirit. In this sense one cannot without difficulty speak of the Spirit as the mutual love of Father and Son, a point Rahner also acknowledges (1974, 106).[72] However, Coffey argues not from this philosophically informed account of the divine essence as is found in Aquinas, but from the economic Trinity, that is, as it is instanced in the mutual love of the Father and the human Jesus. This is most evident in Coffey's argument concerning the love of the Father by the Son where he states: "The sending of the Holy Spirit by Christ is the supreme and all-inclusive primary act of his love of God, i.e. the Father. Flowing as its total act and expression of his humanity endowed in the most radical possible way with the Father's Gift of the Holy Spirit, Spirit of Sonship, Christ's love of the Father is nothing other than the Holy Spirit himself. It corresponds to the bestowal of the Holy Spirit as love by the Son on the Father in the Trinity itself. Thus the relation of the sending of the Holy Spirit by Christ to men to the bestowal of the Holy Spirit by the Son on the Father in the Trinity is evident" (Coffey 1979, 148). Here we see Coffey drawing conclusions from the human will of Christ ("as its total act and expression of his *humanity*") to immanent acts of the Trinity itself. In his later writings he repeats his point: "It is no exaggeration to say that the most basic and important fact revealed in the gospels is the unique love and intimacy obtaining between Jesus and his God" (1999a, 58). Such love, on the part of Jesus, is clearly grounded in the human will of Jesus. It is methodologically unsound to shift from this economic reality to make statements about the immanent Logos. It is at this precise point that Rahner's axiom is most misleading. The blurring of the distinction between the categories of person and nature ends up positing a distinct divine will for the Logos, on the basis of Jesus' human nature.

In relation to Coffey's Trinitarian theology, this is no minor point. Augustine's notion of the Spirit as the mutual love of Father and Son lies at the heart of Coffey's major revision of the Trinitarian relations. It leads to what he calls the "return" or "bestowal" model, as distinct from the "procession" model for understanding those relations. Coffey's revision results in a radical recasting of the *filioque*, an issue I return to later in this chapter.

Problems associated with the application of interpersonal categories to inner-Trinitarian relations are not unique to the work of Rahner and Coffey. Similar problems can be found in the writings of Hans Urs von Balthasar (Doran 2002, 43). This kind of thinking has become widespread, largely under the influence of John Zizioulas' attempt to revive a more Cappadocian style of Trinitarian theology (1985). However attractive such accounts might be, and despite their appeal to the biblical narrative, serious problems remain, even if unacknowledged in much of recent Trinitarian writing. Principle among these is that human interpersonal categories such as love are contingent, freely given, never forced nor necessary. In contrast, the relations constitutive of the divine persons are necessary. If they are not necessary, if these inner-Trinitarian relations are indeed contingent, then inevitably the Son and Spirit should be either conceived as creatures in an Arian sense, or be interpreted as mere historical contingent modes of activity of the deity in a Modalistic manner, or the result is tritheism.[73]

Admittedly this is the key problem of Trinitarian theology. How can we conceive of the person-constituting relations in the Trinity in a way which is personal, but not contingent? How can there be a form of causation which is not impersonal or pre-personal, but at the same time is not a contingent act of will (or acts of wills)? In grappling with such issues the classical psychological analogy demonstrates its real strength. Aquinas describes the procession of the Word in terms of an analogy with the intelligible emanation of the concept from an act of understanding (ST I q27 a1). The analogy here is a form of causation which is both personal and necessary. It is personal inasmuch as the concept proceeds "because" I understand; while it is necessary as an expression of my rational nature. The use of interpersonal categories in dealing with such a problem remains unsuccessful because such categories simply do not display these features. Indeed many modern attempts to do so are barely distinguishable from tritheism.

The *Filioque* in Rahner's Theology

One of the puzzles of Rahner's work on the Trinity is the almost complete absence of any discussion of one of the major elements of Western Trinitarian theology, namely the *filioque*. Perhaps this reflects Rahner's own preference of Eastern over Western approaches to the Trinity, but at no time is this made explicit. The *filioque* makes no appearance in his chapter on the method and structure of the treatise on the triune God. It makes a brief appearance in his chapter on the main lines of magisterial teaching on the Trinity (Rahner 1974, 66). In his third chapter on a systematic outline of Trinitarian theology, he refers to the *taxis* or ordering of the two processions, but it is left to a translator's footnote to clarify, "that is, there is a certain relation of priority and posteriority between the two of them. The Spirit cannot come before the Son" (ibid. 83). There are three or four other mentions of this *taxis* in the remainder of the chapter, but no extended treatment is offered.

At no stage, however, is any reason or ground given for this *taxis*. To all intents and purposes it is simply a brute fact: it "happens to happen" without explanation or underlying reason. Apart from the translator's footnote just referred to, one could just as easily suppose it to be a *spirituque* as a *filioque*. One could get the impression that we have here a basic but formal acceptance of the *filioque*, but one which has little relevance to, or meaning within, Rahner's overall conception of the Trinity. His own characteristic manner of speaking of the two modes of the divine self-communication in Word and Spirit provides no real clues, while attempts to ground the *taxis* in the economic Trinity prove problematic, as the work of both Coffey and Weinandy (1995) illustrates. Indeed Congar criticises Rahner's axiom exactly on this point, since its application to the economy leads to a *spirituque* (1983, 3:11–16). Rahner makes a half-hearted attempt to link the *taxis* with the ordering of knowledge and love; but such reasoning would tend to rely on the very psychological analogy which he has previously dismissed.

We may contrast this with the characteristic Western presentation of the *filioque*, as found in Augustine's *De Trinitate* and Aquinas' *Summa Theologiae*. Augustine's starting point is the Scripture where the Son speaks of sending the Spirit. For Augustine this is a sufficient starting point (DT 4.29). He then moves into a discussion of relations as defining the persons. He notes the asymmetry between the relationship between the Father and the Son and the Spirit: while the Father is father of the Son and the Son is son of the Father, we can say that the Spirit is the spirit of the Father, but not that the Father is father of the Spirit. That would be to understand the Spirit as a second son (DT 5.13). This asymmetry of relationships would suggests that the procession of the Spirit from the Father must also involve the Son; hence the *filioque* with its implication of the Father and the Son being one origin of the Holy Spirit (DT 5.15). Aquinas argues in similar fashion such that: "Therefore we must conclude that it is necessary to say that either the Son is from the Holy Spirit [i.e. *spirituque!*]; which no one says; or that the Holy Spirit is from the Son, as we confess" (ST I q36 a2). The theological argument is in fact a logical clarification based on the notion of persons as defined by relations. It is a deduction from previously settled principles, but which in itself adds no further understanding. Its truth should be seen as the logical outcome of the principles from which it is drawn. But this judgment leaves the mind still seeking further understanding.

To achieve this both Augustine and Aquinas move beyond logical clarification to some analogous intelligibility through the use of a psychological analogy. For Augustine "nothing is loved which is not first known" (DT 8.6, 9.3, 10.2). Aquinas elucidates this psychological observation with a more precise formulation: "nothing can be loved by the will unless it is conceived in the intellect" (ST I q27 a3). With this observation both theologians move beyond the certainty of a judgment made on principles to an understanding based on an analogy drawn from our conscious human acts of knowing and loving. Such an understanding remains analogous and is indeed hypothetical in its application to the divine Trinity. It does not provide a proof nor satisfy the criteria of necessity, but it does satisfy theological inquiry, as faith seeks some understanding, albeit analogous.

Again we can grasp the gap between the two theological projects we have been considering. Rahner rejects the psychological analogy on the very grounds that it fails to do what it never tries to do. It cannot prove the necessity of the divine processions and the distinction of persons. It remains hypothetical. As noted above, for Rahner the theological goal is the necessary—faith seeking necessary reasons—not a modest and reverent understanding—*fides quaerens intellectum*, to follow Anselm's dictum. Following Rahner's lead, Coffey goes so far as to suggest that the psychological analogy does not even qualify as theology proper. It is merely an "illustration" (Coffey 1999a, 4).

Now it seems to be something of a law that, where the intelligibility of a powerful theological synthesis is no longer grasped, then theologians will attempt new syntheses which begin by dismissing the previous achievement and end with a denial of the facts or doctrines one was originally seeking to synthesise. This suggestion is indeed made by Bernard Lonergan who argues that "first, the system can be poorly understood; second, it can be rejected out of hand; third the very facts that it would understand can be denied" (Doran 2001, 79).[74] It is clear that the theological synthesis achieved by Aquinas has extraordinary explanatory power. The psychological analogy is an intrinsic component of that synthesis. It provides, among other things, a coherent and critical intelligibility in regard to the *filioque*. Rahner has moved decisively away from Aquinas' synthesis in general, and distanced himself from the psychological analogy in particular. But without the analogy, the *filioque* becomes a brute fact, a mere happens-to-happen, but with no intelligibility of its own. It is inevitable then that later theologians, building on Rahner, will similarly be left stranded, as is the case with Coffey, and a number of other theologians as well.

Coffey has engaged in a long-term project to reconceptualise the inner Trinitarian relationships through what he often calls the bestowal or return model. As we noted above this is developed as a systematisation of the Augustinian account of the Spirit as the mutual love of the Father and the Son. Coffey speaks of two distinct models, the more familiar "procession model," which "assumed definitive form in the psychological model"; and a second model derived from the Augustinian position, in which the Spirit is the love of the Father for the Son and the answering love of the Son for the Father. Coffey considers these two as being based on "two irreducible Trinitarian data" so that no harmonising synthesis is necessary, or possible (1979; 1984, 470–71; 1986, 230–35; 1999a, 46–65). The fact that no synthesis is even possible suggests that these models are simply human constructs projected onto a fundamentally unintelligible reality, in a Kantian mode, as I argued in Chapter 4. Nonetheless Coffey finds the bestowal model far more theologically fruitful, a better way of dealing with problems in Christology and the theology of grace. Indeed Coffey refers to the procession model as inadequate, unsatisfactory and narcissistic (1999a, 60). Again we see the eliding of the procession account and the psychological analogy. The procession account is simply an account of persons and their relations, while the analogy adds the psychological dimension to these. It is the psychological dimension that Coffey finds "narcissistic." Within his process of reconceptualisation the *filioque* certainly has no privileged place. It arises only in one "model," whose status is further compromised through its identification with the "psychological model."

Coffey has further sought to clarify his position in relation to the *filioque* in an article written in response to a document from the Pontifical Council for Promoting Christian Unity, a document which sought to build bridges between Catholic and Orthodox positions on the procession of the Holy Spirit (Coffey 2003).[75] In it he introduces the distinction between Trinitarian statements *in fieri* ('in becoming') and *in facto esse* ('in constituted being'). Coffey reads the classical doctrine of processions as statements *in fieri*, while his own bestowal model is to be read *in facto esse*. He regards the introduction of such time-conditioned language as "inevitable" in dealing with the processions. Moreover to attempt to reconcile these two perspectives is to betray a "rationalism of the kind against which the East constantly and reasonably protests." The *filioque* is a statement *in fieri*, not *in facto esse* (ibid. 16–18).

One can see the same sort of outcome in the Trinitarian writings of Thomas Weinandy, in particular his book *The Father's Spirit of Sonship*. Weinandy proposes that "the Father begets the Son in the Spirit and thus that the Spirit proceeds from the Father as the one in whom the Son is begotten and so in turn proceeds from the Son as the one in whom and through whom the Son loves the Father" (1995, 89). Here we find both a relativising of the *filioque* and an attempt to use interpersonal categories in an account of the relationship of Father and Son. In relation to the psychological analogy he views its "Aristotelian epistemology as detrimental to a true understanding of the Trinity." Indeed, a "proper understanding of the Trinity can only be obtained if all three persons, logically and ontologically, spring forth in one simultaneous, nonsequential, eternal act in which each person of the Trinity subsistently defines, and equally is subsistently defined by, the other persons" (ibid. 14–15). (To his credit, however, Weinandy does seem to recognise the role of the analogy as providing an understanding, not as a determiner of necessary facts.) The same direction can be found in the work of Leonardo Boff, *Trinity and Society*. Boff seeks to relativises the *filioque* by the addition of a *spirituque*, for the sake of "Trinitarian balance" (1988, 204–6).

Though some might find this de-emphasis on the *filioque* more ecumenically helpful, it is difficult to know whether these radical suggestions will find any resonance within the Orthodox tradition. They do however illustrate how the *filioque* has been increasingly found to be unintelligible within contemporary theology. As long as it appears to be nothing more than a brute fact, it is inevitable that its very facticity should be denied or at least relativised.

The Question of Method

I have already made some preliminary comments about the issue of theological method. I would now like to expand on those comments by raising a basic question: What is the goal of theology? Differing answers to this question highlight major differences between Rahner, on the one side, and Augustine and Aquinas on the other.

I have already observed above that Rahner's major criticism of the psychological analogy is that it remains hypothetical. It cannot be proven to be the case. It is unscriptural, except on the basis of artificial "eisegesis." It cannot explain the transition from essential to notional acts (Rahner 1974, 19). I have suggested above that Rahner's primary focus here is on what is necessarily the case. An example of this is his insistence that only the Logos may be incarnated. He thereby rejects the opinion of Aquinas. What seems to lie behind this is a conception of theology that is concerned with uncovering what is necessarily so, that is, a concern with certainty. When that concern dominates, the goal of theology becomes the careful ascertaining of the "facts," that is, what we know to definitely be the case because it is necessarily so. How does one go about uncovering the facts? One begins with the Scriptures, the early Church Councils and the Fathers, preferably the Greek ones (ibid. 58). From these facts one may deduce more facts and so constitute theological progress.

This standard of certainty and necessity is very high and, measured against it, the psychological analogy will inevitably fail. But then Rahner's own performance fares little better. In Chapter 3 of *The Trinity*, where he develops an outline for a systematics, Rahner identifies a fourfold "group of aspects" to promote a better grasp of the Trinitarian mystery. These emerge from the analysis of divine self-communication: (a) Origin-Future; (b) History-Transcendence; (c) Invitation (offer)-Acceptance; (d) Knowledge-Love (ibid. 94–95). It is hard to see how these are any less hypothetical than the psychological analogy, and indeed the final pair of aspects clearly relates to it.

Again the work of Coffey is illustrative of this same concern with certainty. His comments on Augustine's *De Trinitate* are informative. Having rejected the psychological analogy as a mere "illustration," he defends Augustine, despite his origination of the analogy, because at least "the first seven [books of *De Trinitate*] are devoted to the mystery of the Trinity in itself," whereas only the later section is devoted to the analogy (Coffey 1999a, 4). An examination of the first seven books reveals that it is concerned with establishing the Trinitarian mystery from Scripture and clarifying it in terms of categories of relation, person, essence and substance. It is concerned with establishing the "facts" of the Trinity. As far as Coffey is concerned the rest of the work moves away from this proper purpose of theology. Yet Augustine ends Book 7 with one of his favourite biblical texts, "Unless you believe, you will not understand." For Augustine the first seven books are concerned with establishing what is to be believed. By quoting this text Augustine signals to us that the proper theological task of understanding is now about to begin.

Overall the Western theological tradition has viewed the goal of theology not as certainty and necessity but as understanding. The Anselmian adage of "faith seeking understanding" was prefigured in the Augustinian precept, "Believe, in order that you may understand" (see DT 7.12). (One should of course acknowledge that while Anselm spoke of theology as "faith seeking understanding," his own theological approach often sought "necessary reasons" as in *Cur Deus Homo?*) For Aquinas, understanding of the doctrines of faith is the pre-eminent goal of theology. While faith terminates in a personal relationship with God, it is mediated to the believer through the cognitive meaning found in the Scriptures and the teaching of the Church (ST II-II q1 a2). To settle matters of faith one appeals to an authority; to settle matters of understanding one turns to a teacher (*Quodlibetal Questions* IV q9a3 [18])(Ogilvie 2001, 138).

Within this framework the goal of theology is to add intelligibility to scripturally and dogmatically ascertained "facts." This is precisely the purpose of the psychological analogy adopted by Augustine and refined by Aquinas. It is not that Scripture or Church teaching warrants it. Rather it systematises and renders intelligible, at least analogously so, what Scripture and Church teaching present to us for belief. In more recent time this framework has been grounded by Lonergan in the cognitional distinction between judgment and understanding, to form the basis of his distinction between the functional specialties of doctrine and systematics (Lonergan 1972).[76] The same approach can be found in Vatican I's constitution *De Filius*, which posited the goal for theology as the fruitful understanding of the mysteries of faith from analogies of what is naturally known and through interconnection of the mysteries themselves and with our final end (DS 3016). The hypothetical character of this process, to which Rahner objects, is in fact essential, for otherwise one would be proving mysteries of the faith by reason alone, a criticism levelled at the analogy by Karl Barth (1936, 1/1:383–84).

Again we can illustrate the difference between these two theological worlds by reference to the work of Coffey. For Coffey the account of the Trinity based on the processions is a model, one which he finds inadequate and seeks to supersede with a better model, that of bestowal. Both can be viewed as alternative accounts of equal standing, both interpretations of scriptural facts, whose relative merits are open to further theological evaluation. However, for both Augustine and Aquinas the processions are not an interpretation of scripture; they are dogmatically given facts, judgments made by the Church in its exposition of the meaning of the Scriptures. As such they are to be found in the Nicene Creed. They are then dogmatic judgments or facts which theology seeks to render intelligible, lest the mind be starved of understanding. Augustine would be aghast to think that his speculative notion of the Spirit as mutual love of the Father and Son should be used to supplant the dogmatically certain notion of processions of the Son and Spirit from the Father.[77]

Conclusion

The further contemporary theology moves away from the distinction between dogmatic and systematic issues, the more the "facts" of dogmatic theology become unintelligible and increasingly subject to disputation. The widespread collapse of the type of authority that Aquinas appealed to for settling dogmatic disputes has resulted in theological syntheses, which reflect more and more the personal preferences of their authors. Some find in this situation a healthy pluralism, while others might judge it to reflect an intellectual individualism whose concern is more to forge a new path rather than walk the well-worn road of a previous heritage. However we read it contemporary Trinitarian theology has moved a long way from the Western tradition.

It is not at all clear that Rahner would be happy with the multiple paths Trinitarian theology has taken from the starting point he suggested. But, at the same time, much of it might find its origins in his incomplete appreciation of the Western tradition on the Trinity, hindered perhaps by its neo-Scholastic mediators. Certainly there were problems with this mediation, as noted by Lonergan (1997).

But the solution may lie more in a proper appropriation of the past, rather than its benign neglect. Such is the thesis of this present work. As Dallavalle notes, "left with Rahner, Trinitarian theology could easily end up as impoverished as he saw it to be in the manuals of neo-scholasticism" (1998, 150). It may seem a harsh judgment, but the warning signs are evident.

Chapter 7
The Future for (Trinitarian) Theology

It is clear that we no longer live in the same intellectual, ecclesial and cultural world as that of Augustine and Aquinas. Christendom emerged to stand on the shoulders of Augustine and, of all Christendom's children, none penetrated more deeply into the Christian mysteries than Thomas Aquinas. But Christendom is long gone and no amount of romantic longing can bring it back. Its own inner tensions helped bring about its downfall resulting in the Reformation, the Enlightenment, modernity and now post-modernity. If the Reformation sowed the theological seeds of a suspicion of reason, the Enlightenment philosophy of Kant ensured its full flowering. Reason, Kant proclaimed, could not reach the noumenal reality of things. Human acts of meaning, interpretation and understanding were no longer to be thought of as doorways to reality. They were simply human constructs projected onto a noumenal reality that remained forever beyond our reach. The cognitional value of rationality was cast into significant doubt.

Despite this sundering of knowledge and reality, this lack of confidence in the cognitional powers of the mind, Kant remained strangely assured that universal reason could provide a sure guide for practical, ethical matters. Soon enough this assurance evaporated as the competing claims of various philosophers to establish a universal moral code from reason alone were subject to modernity's hermeneutics of suspicion. For Marx these claims were nothing but reflections of the class interests of their creators; for Freud they represented the struggle of the superego to control the urgings of our baser instincts; for Nietzsche these claims can be reduced to an expression of the will to power. No longer could the rationality of value be assumed. Now in our post-modern world, all forms of life, of culture and tradition are equally unfounded myths, a thesis propounded by John Milbank (1991). All truth claims are now nothing more that an exercise of the will to power, needing to be unmasked by a suitable hermeneutic of suspicion. Some theological approaches, such as the radical orthodoxy of Milbank, have embraced these post-modern positions, since they seem to recognise a valid place for religion in societies where it had been increasingly marginalised by secularism. However, these same events may also be read as symptoms of cultural decline, something which needs our urgent concern, not our enthusiastic embrace.

Still, the task of addressing this history of decline is far from easy. Consider the impact of this history on the Western tradition of Trinitarian theology. Once we lose basic positions such as the value of rationality and the rationality of value the psychological analogy is weakened to vague statements about "knowledge and love." Its deep inner coherence no longer illuminates either the human or the divine reality. It is met with little more than a shrug of the shoulders, as just a surface description of human experience. It can no longer provide a profound intelligibility to the Trinitarian beliefs of faith. Stripped of the intelligibility provided by the psychological analogy these beliefs become an odd collection of almost mathematical facts, "five characteristics, four relations, three persons, two processions, one God and no proof" (O'Collins 1999, 147). Little wonder then that contemporary theologians have sought to distance themselves from the Western tradition. Most have absorbed the post-Kantian ethos, some unwittingly, but some explicitly and willingly.

For anyone seeking to revive or revitalise the Western tradition there is a massive task of cultural transformation to be undertaken. One cannot rekindle interest in that tradition without reasserting the cultural assumptions that constitute its field of meaning. And as I noted in Chapter 4, that may be part of the point of the Trinitarian revelation. Revelation forces us to be cultural change agents at this level of profound philosophical engagement. This is evident not only in terms of the doctrine of the Trinity, but also in relation to the theology of grace where profound questions of human freedom are raised. As Lonergan has argued, "the hopeless tangle ... of endlessly multiplied philosophies, is not merely a *cul-de-sac* for human progress; it is also a reign of sin, a despotism of darkness; and men are its slaves" (1992, 714). This critical philosophical engagement by theology is part of the redemptive process initiated by revelation.

John Paul II's encyclical *Fides et ratio* supports a similar view with regard to impact of revelation on philosophy. There we find that

"Revelation therefore introduces into our history a universal and ultimate truth which stirs the human mind to ceaseless effort; indeed it impels reason continually to extend the range of its knowledge until it senses that it has done all in its power, leaving no stone unturned" (FR n.14). Indeed sections of Chapter 4 of the encyclical read like an unfolding narrative of the ways in which faith has stirred the human minds in developing and sustaining an ongoing tradition of rationality, culminating in the contribution of Aquinas: "It is therefore minimising and mistaken to restrict their work simply to the transposition of the truths of faith into philosophical categories. They did much more. In fact they succeeded in disclosing completely all that remained implicit and preliminary in the thinking of the great philosophers of antiquity" (FR n.41). The encyclical would go so far as to see this emerging tradition of rationality as part of the divine providential plan: "The Church cannot abandon what she has gained from her inculturation in the world of Greco-Latin thought. To reject this heritage would be to deny the providential plan of God who guides the Church down the paths of time and history" (FR n.72). John Paul II clearly envisages the position that revelation has such a cultural impact through its engagement with philosophical issues.

It is on the question of revelation that it is possible to discern two distinctive, perhaps even dialectically opposed, fundamental positions within contemporary theology. While most theologians may never clarify precisely where they stand in relation to these two positions, and so hover between them, they represent fundamental options leading to totally different conceptions of the theological task.

The first position is reflective of the Kantian separation of interpretation and fact, meaning and reality. Its characteristic categories are those of experience and interpretation. We experience reality, which is then subject to our interpretation. However, this interpretive process is "projective," a construct or model that never captures the truth of the reality experienced. Reality offers "permanent resistance ... to our rational inventions [forcing] us to constantly new and untried models of thought" (Schillebeeckx 1980, 22).[78] While this permanent resistance applies to all our experiences of reality, it applies even more so with our experiences of the divine reality. All our talk about God becomes so many faltering and failing attempts to give expression to our basic experience of the divine. Religious language, and particularly theological language as a specialised form of religious language, is always symbolic and metaphorical (Haight 1999, 8–12). Any cognitive function of meaning is denied, to be replaced by poetic, narrative and rhetorical forms.

Good examples of the endpoint of such a trajectory can be found in the writings of Roger Haight and John Hick. In his seminal article, "The Case for Spirit Christology" (1992), Haight seeks to develop a Christology that takes seriously the work of the Spirit of God. But the language of Spirit does not refer to the third person of the Trinity. Rather the Spirit of God is a biblical symbol referring "to God from a certain point of view; it indicates God as active, and as power, energy or force … God present and at work outside of God's self, in the world of God's creation" (ibid. 266–67). Talk of God's spirit is simply a way of speaking of the divine immanence to creation. There are in fact a number of biblical symbols of divine immanence that "appear to be interchangeable" (ibid. 267). And when it comes to the question of the incarnation, the language of Logos is just another symbol of God's presence and activity in Jesus. Its adoption by Nicea "does not entail a ratification of the symbol of the Logos … the precise doctrine of Nicaea is not an affirmation of the Logos itself … Thus the doctrine of Nicaea can be paraphrased in this way: not less than God was present to and operative in Jesus" (ibid. 274). Given the interchangeability of symbols of divine immanence, one might as well speak about a Spirit Christology as a Logos Christology. The fact that the Trinity of three persons in one God has been replaced by a binity of transcendence-immanence is of no major concern, because all religious language is symbolic anyway. As I noted in Chapter 1, the end result is clear. In Haight's account, in good Kantian fashion, the intra-divine is a completely inaccessible realm so that any reference to an immanent Trinity is a leftover from dogmatic and Scholastic theology (1999, 487).

The same Kantian presuppositions can be found in the writings of John Hick, who seeks to relativise the truth claims of all religious traditions, putting them on an equal footing (1974; 1985; 1993; 1995). Hick tells the parable of the blind people encountering an elephant. Each gives a very different description of the encounter, depending on what part of the elephant each touches. But they are all encountering the same reality. Different religions are like those blind people, each encountering the one reality and giving a different account (Hick 1974, 260). However, the nature of this one reality becomes more and more obscure. Initially Hick opted for a general theism, but Buddhists are not always theistic, so he moved to calling it "ultimate reality." Whether this reality was personal or impersonal was an open question. In the end this trajectory understands all religions as so much human reaching up to the divine. The notion that God might enter into human history to reveal Godself is methodologically ruled out, precisely because it seems to privilege one segment of history over all others. Traditional Christological and Trinitarian doctrine, grounded in the historical revelation of Jesus Christ, become just religious symbols rather than true faith affirmations. In his own way Hick has replicated the journey of modernity, from Christian faith, to deism, to an inevitable agnosticism.[79]

Now it is unlikely that most theologians would embrace these conclusions. Such conclusions stand at significant variance to the faith, as it has been traditionally understood. Yet in many ways they are the logical outcome of the presuppositions from which these theologians often operate. And these presuppositions are widely disseminated if not always explicitly adopted. Unless a theologian critically assesses these presuppositions and creates a personal distance from them, he or she is unlikely to be able to resist the logic of the final conclusions.

In the Western tradition we find a very different conception of our relationship to the divine. The categories are no longer experience and interpretation, but truth and meaning. Revelation is not just some passive experience of the divine. Rather, it is initiated by God who desires to communicate something of the divine reality to us. God reveals and God is trustworthy; God can neither deceive nor be deceived. God's self-communication is the entry of divine (and hence true) meanings and values into human history. These meanings and values are redemptive; they turn us away from falsehood and self-deception and towards truth and goodness. The most profound entry of divine meaning is the incarnation, whereby the divine person of the Logos enters into human history. As incarnate divine meaning Jesus Christ is himself the fullness of God's self-communication to human history. In order that the impact of this divine meaning not be lost to human history, the providential mercy of God ensures that this meaning is maintained as a saving reality until the end of time through the work of the Spirit. Within this providential history "the word of religious expression is not just the objectification of the gift of God's love; in a privileged area it also is specific meaning, the word of God himself" (Lonergan 1972, 119). Christians, at least until the modern era, have recognised the Scriptures and, to some extent, the doctrines of the great Church Councils as belonging to this privileged area of meaning. On this position the great councils do not present us with yet another interpretation in the endless cycles of interpretation and reinterpretation; rather they are judgments of truth seeking to preserve the divine meaning present in the incarnation, mission, death and resurrection of Jesus (ibid. 295–333).

While the first position blurs the distinction between the task of the theologian and the decrees of the Church, which are viewed as just another theological interpretation, the second account understands that there is indeed a proper distinction between the theological task of understanding the faith and the ecclesial responsibility of defining the faith. Theology is subsumed within this ecclesial responsibility. Specifically, the concern of systematic theology "is a promotion of the being, and good systematic theology a promotion of the well-being, of meaning, and indeed of that meaning that is the outer word of God in history" (Doran 1990, 629). Thus theology helps ensure the well-being of the tradition of rationality initiated, sustained and prolonged by divine revelation (Ormerod 2000). Within that tradition, at least in its Western form, Augustine and Aquinas have played a pivotal role.

However, there remain two major roadblocks on the path to the elaboration of theology as so conceived within our post-modern world. The first is the emergence of historical consciousness. What has given credence to the shift from the classical conception of theology to the more recent post-Kantian conception has been the strong realisation of the social, cultural and historical context of all discourse. The work of critical historical studies, combined with various hermeneutics of suspicion, has undermined any contender for a privileged area of meaning, be it the Scriptures, Church Councils, or the early Church

Fathers. In response to this, Joseph Ratzinger identified as a central problem for contemporary theology the need to find "a better synthesis between historical and theological methods, between higher criticism and church doctrine." Further, "a truly pervasive understanding of this whole problem has yet to be found which takes into account both the undeniable insights uncovered by historical method, while at the same time overcoming its limitations" (Ratzinger 1988, 596). Bernard Lonergan too has stated, "The whole problem in modern theology, Protestant and Catholic, is the introduction of historical scholarship" (Crowe 1992, 98). Indeed, Lonergan's major work, *Method in Theology*, is the culmination of a lifetime's struggle to provide a solution to this problem of introducing historical scholarship while being faithful to the doctrines of the past. The eight functional specialties of his method—research, interpretation, history, dialectics, foundations, doctrines, systematics and communications—provide an integrated collaborative framework for combining historical scholarship with fidelity to tradition.

This brings us to a second problem. Lonergan's achievement is predicated on the attainment of what he calls the third stage of meaning (1972, 85–96). This stage of meaning is attained when one can differentiate and relate the three realms of meaning, commonsense, theory and interiority. Only a move into the realm of interior meaning can ground the necessary transcultural meanings and values that can transcend the relativism which threatens to evacuate doctrines of any permanent significance. Indeed initial steps in this direction can be found in Augustine and Aquinas. Augustine recognised the heuristic function of the term "person," when he noted, "So we say three persons, not in order to say that precisely, but in order not to be reduced to silence" (DT 5.10). Aquinas went further to identify key Trinitarian terminology with the questioning intentionality of the subject: "Therefore the divine essence is signified as 'What?'; and the person as 'Who?'; and the property as 'Whereby?'" (ST I q32 a2). A move to the interior realm of meaning can ground the key doctrinal distinctions between person and nature/essence not in some metaphysical theory but it the inner dynamics of questioning (Ormerod 1993b).

As I argued in Chapter 3, Augustine in precocious fashion achieved the type of differentiation I have just described in *De Trinitate*. His work maintains a clear distinction between commonsense (Books 1–4), theoretic (Books 5–7) and interior (Books 8–11) modes of argumentation. Such a differentiation is not even maintained in the work of Aquinas, who, in the scientific mode of the day, presented even the psychological analogy in terms of the theoretical realm of Aristotelian metaphysics. Much contemporary theology, on the other hand, can scarcely distinguish biblical commonsense from philosophical theory, while the realm of interiority is treated either in commonsense fashion or as yet another theoretic mode of discourse. Such an undifferentiated eclecticism is unlikely to be able to appreciate the achievements of the Western tradition, let alone bring them into constructive dialogue with the needs of the present.

Books 12–15 of Augustine's *De Trinitate*, however, are a reminder that the cognitive function of meaning, with all its intellectual asceticism, is not the only mode of Trinitarian discourse. Here Augustine invites his readers to join him in the praise and glory of God, Father, Son and Spirit. In this way he recognised that people need to be moved by the belief in the triune God (effective meaning); they need a sense of identity as persons called to communion with that God (constitutive meaning); and they need their faith communicated to them in ways that capture their minds *and* their imaginations (communicative meaning). However, these functions of meaning have generally not been well developed in the Western tradition. In Chapter 5 I argued that the classical doctrine of appropriations may be read as one way of expanding Trinitarian discourse beyond the cognitive function of meaning to embrace other functions as well. There are dangers in this approach, particularly if the other functions of meaning are too far removed from the cognitive function. As Doran notes, "to the extent that one has not yet distinguished insight and judgment from sensitive and imaginative experience, one regards the real as 'the object of a sufficiently integrated and sufficiently intense flow of sensitive representations, feelings, words, and actions' (*I*:538); and to that extent one either becomes a creator of myths or falls victim to other myth-makers" (Doran 1990, 193). Without serious attention to and grounding in the cognitive function of meaning, Christian belief in the Trinity will become just another religious myth in a growing post-modern market place of such myths. If that were to happen, the well-being of the outer word of God in history would not be well served by Christian theologians.

This exploration of other functions of meaning besides the cognitive, while avoiding the dangers of myth-making, is not the only task confronting the future of Trinitarian theology. Throughout this work I have consistently identified the pivotal role played by the psychological analogy within the Western tradition, and argued for the need to reappropriate the analogy in the modern context. This task is ongoing and this present essay is, I hope, a contribution to it. However, in the terms of Vatican I, this is only part of the theological task. For theology must not only find fruitful analogies for divine mysteries in the created order, it must also find interconnections between those mysteries and with our eschatological end.

Initial, if flawed, attempts to move in this direction were undertaken by Karl Rahner (see Chapter 6). Beginning with his reflections on the beatific vision, Rahner developed his notion of quasi-formal causality to give metaphysical expression to the divine self-communication of Word and Spirit present in the incarnation and grace. He based his account of divine self-communication on the two processions, and so identified two distinct forms of self-communication. The beatific vision was viewed as the completion of the life of grace, which involved a real communication of the Spirit, while the incarnation remained a distinct form of communication of the Word (Coffey 1979, 56–58). Under the pressure to develop a unified account of grace, Coffey seeks to collapse even this relatively undifferentiated scheme through the development of a "Spirit Christology," which blurs the distinction between the communication of the Word and that of the Spirit. In particular, Coffey is responding to the criticism of Karl Barth, that the Catholic theology of grace "has not succeeded in overcoming the dichotomy between men and Christ" by identifying "the principal grace of Christ [as] the grace of union, while the principal grace of men is the Holy Spirit" (1979, 1). Nonetheless Rahner's instinctive desire for some form of unification of these major doctrinal beliefs was sound.

Bernard Lonergan has provided a more differentiated schema. Rather than take as his starting point the two processions, Lonergan begins with the four relations that correspond with the two processions:

there are four real divine relations, really identical with divine being, and so four special ways of grounding an imitation or participation *ad extra* of God's own life. And there are four absolutely supernatural created realities. They are never found in an unformed or indeterminate state. They are: the secondary act of existence of the Incarnation, sanctifying grace, the habit of charity, and the light of glory.

Thus it can appropriately be maintained that the secondary act of existence of the Incarnation is a created participation of paternity, and so that it has a special relation to the Son; that sanctifying grace is a [created] participation of active spiration, and so that it bears a special relation to the Holy Spirit; that the habit of charity is a [created] participation of passive spiration, and so that it has a special relation to the Father and the Son; and that the light of glory is a [created] participation of filiation that leads perfectly the children of adoption back to the Father.[80]

Such a schema keeps differing realities properly distinct, such as the beatific vision from grace and the incarnation from grace, while also adding distinctions within grace between sanctifying grace and the habit of charity, a distinction which Rahner's scheme tends to obscure. From this perspective the doctrine of the Trinity provides what Doran identifies as a "unified field structure" for a systematic account of these basic Christian mysteries.[81] A fuller explication of this structure is another task for theology in the future.

Rahner was certainly correct in identifying problems in the Trinitarian faith of ordinary believers, and the decadence into which neo-Scholastic Trinitarian theology had fallen. Certainly contemporary theology has witnessed an explosion of works that attempt to correct the deficiencies. But like Rahner himself, their appropriation of the Western tradition leaves something to be desired. My hope is that this book has at the least brought that tradition back into the conversation, at a time when its voice has been struggling to be heard.

Notes

1 Yves Congar notes and rejects the claims made by Vladimir Lossky concerning the ecclesiological impact of the *filioque* (Congar 1983, 3:208–11). Nonetheless some Catholic authors do assert a connection between the *filioque* and papal primacy, for example, Bertrand de Margerie (1982, 176), "As the Spirit is bound to Christ and dependent on him, so the *Filioque* ... is bound to the papacy."

2 Rahner does not claim the axiom as an original creation, and there are antecedents, but it is now clearly identified with his thought.

3 The writings of John Milbank are representative of an era that has lost faith in the intelligibility of reality. For Milbank, all discourse is rhetorical, an instance of the will to power; all foundational claims are suspect and all metaphysics are master narratives, unfounded myths that we either accept or reject on rhetorical grounds (1991).

4 Terms such as essence, nature and substance, and person and *hypostasis* are interchangeable precisely because they operate heuristically, that is, they name an otherwise unknown as "to-be-known." Efforts to make precise distinctions between them fail to recognise their heuristic significance.

5 For a brief history of the introducing of the *filioque* into the creed, as well as Orthodox objections, see Edmund Hill (1985, 108–20).

6 A good example of this is the manner in which Aquinas deals with the question of the *filioque*, in ST I q36 a2. He begins by quoting authority, in this instance the Athanasian Creed (unaware, of course, of the historical difficulties associated with this), then presents an analysis in terms of relations, and concludes with the analogous argument based on the psychological analogy.

7 See Schillebeeckx (1990, 43): "earlier expressions of faith, even dogmas, are on the one hand irrevocable and irreversible: they cannot be done away with, since with a particular social and cultural system of reference they have time and again expressed and sought to safeguard the mystery of Jesus Christ ... in a way which is sometimes more and sometimes less successful for that time. But on the other hand, in their cultural and historical forms they can become irrelevant and indeed meaningless for later generations as

they are simply repeated as they stand, because earlier generations expressed their deepest convictions about Christian faith within another semantic field, in another system of communication, and through a different perspective on reality."

[8] Augustine provides several analogies, but it is the one developed in DT Book 9 that provides Aquinas with the insight he needs for his later systematisation.

[9] Augustine was confident that his readers could verify what he is talking about in developing the psychological analogy, through an examination of their own conscious experience; see DT 9.3.

[10] See Robert M. Doran (1990, 193): "But to the extent that one has not yet distinguished insight and judgment from sensitive and imaginative experience, one regards the real as 'the object of a sufficiently integrated and sufficiently intense flow of sensitive representations, feelings, words, and actions' (*I*:538); and to that extent one either becomes a creator of myths or falls victim to other myth-makers." The inner quote is from Lonergan (1958, 538).

[11] See, for example, Leslie Dewart (1966; 1969). Dewart describes Harnack's position in the following terms: "The early development of Christian doctrine is to be understood as the gradual *substitution* of Hellenic elements for the corresponding original elements of the Apostolic Church, and the accumulation of these changes amounts ... to a substantial change in Christian truth" (1969, 106).

[12] One of the better analyses of the whole question of divine suffering can be found in Thomas G. Weinandy (1999). Weinandy argues for the greater intellectual coherence of the Western tradition on this point.

[13] For criticisms of Rahner's axiom, see Congar (1983, 3:11–16) and Kasper (1984, 273–277). Both accept the epistemological claim but have reservations about any possible metaphysical claim that would eliminate reference to an immanent Trinity.

[14] The review by Joseph DiNoia (1993, 214–216) expresses concerns that LaCugna's work undermines the reality of the immanent Trinity. Joseph Bracken expresses similar concerns in his review (1992, 558–560). Also see Nancy Dallavalle (1998, esp. 148–149).

[15] As Rahner notes, "the differentiation of the self-communication of God in history (of truth) and spirit (of love) must belong to God

'in himself'. Or otherwise this difference, which undoubtedly exists, would do away with God's *self*-communication" (1974, 100). As is well known, Karl Barth also posits an intimate connection between God's Trinitarian nature and the process of revelation.

[16] An excellent account of Balthasar's complex Trinitarian thought can be found in Anne Hunt (1997, esp. 57–89).

[17] As Doran argues, the issue is one of the relationship between, and deployment of, what Lonergan calls general and special categories. Special categories arise from the faith tradition and refer to religious realities, while general categories arise from philosophy, social sciences and other disciplines. Ecclesiologies based on Trinitarian theology draw almost exclusively on special categories to the neglect of, or even hostility to, general categories, drawn, for example, from the social sciences (1997, 61–84).

[18] This is a charge regularly made concerning the Trinitarian writings of Moltmann; see O'Donnell (1988, 108). Moltmann's follower, Volf, in fact explicitly rejects the notion of "one numerically identical nature" (1998, 203). It is difficult to see how this could be anything but tritheistic.

[19] While Lonergan only wrote occasional pieces on the Trinity in English, he did write substantial works in Latin for the use of his students at the Gregorianum University. I shall mainly draw on Lonergan's *Verbum* and *Method*.

[20] This chapter is a revised version of an earlier journal article by Ormerod (2003a).

[21] The article was subsequently reprinted in Gunton (1997, 31–57).

[22] See Michael René Barnes (1995; 1999); John C. Cavadini (1992; 1997); Lewis Ayres (1998); Basil Studer (1997); and Johannes Brachtendorf (1998).

[23] Quoted in Barnes (1999, 152).

[24] Note however that this statement does not reflect Cavadini's own understanding of Augustine. Like myself, Cavadini rejects such a characterisation.

[25] All my quotes from *De Trinitate* are taken from the translation by Edmund Hill. See Augustine (1991). However where Gunton has quoted Augustine, I have been faithful to his translation.

[26] See the articles referred to in n.21 above.

[27] One might note that previously Gunton criticises Augustine for not having the Word substantially present in OT theophanies while here he complains that the Spirit is substantially present in the whole life of Jesus. There is an inconsistency here that reflects a relatively ad hoc methodology in Gunton's work.

[28] Translation from Henry Bettenson (1970, 117).

[29] Gregory of Nyssa also makes a sharp distinction between "intellectual existence" and the "sensible world," favouring the former over the latter in seeking to understanding the nature of divinity and the Trinity; see *Contra Eunomium* 1.22 from Bettenson (1970, 155–157).

[30] It should be noted that in saying this Basil is concurring with Augustine precisely where Gunton sees opposition between them. As Gunton provides no source for his assertion regarding Basil, his assertion regarding Basil cannot be verified.

[31] Translation from Bettenson (1970, 81). Gregory of Nyssa gives his own version as well: "The only distinction here is that the Father is father, not son: the Son is son, not father; similarly the Holy Spirit is neither father nor son" (Bettenson 1970, 158).

[32] See for example, Volf, who explicitly rejects the notion of "one numerically identical nature" (1998, 203).

[33] In this regard I found Brachtendorf's attempts (1998) to untangle Augustine's position on faith and understanding not particularly helpful.

[34] Translation from (Bettenson 1970, 151).

[35] Stevenson (2000) provides a convincing argument as to why, after an initial attempt, Aquinas rejects the analogy of memory, understanding and will, and turns to the analogy based on intelligible emanations, as found in ST I q27. As for significance of the terminology of memory in Augustine's text, see Salvino Biolo (1979).

[36] Translation from (Bettenson 1970, 154).

[37] The major exception to this is the work of Brachtendorf (1998), cited above, which is contains a summary of his larger work (2000).

[38] One might be tempted to posit a dependence of Lonergan on Augustine, given the parallels are so close. However, in his extended treatment of self-knowledge in Lonergan, *Verbum*, 87–99, all the references are to Aristotle and Aquinas. It seems just as likely that

these four thinkers come to the same position because they are attending to the same facts about human consciousness. For a Lonerganian reading of Augustine see Biolo (1979).

[39] I would like to suggest that this last sentence it better translated as "That the mind knows itself in part and does not in part know itself?" I think Augustine may be seeking to distinguish between a partial knowing (of the whole) and a knowing of a part (of the whole).

[40] This chapter is a revised version of an earlier journal article by Ormerod (2003b).

[41] Commentators are divided over how much of Book 12 Augustine had completed before the work was stolen.

[42] For a summary of some of its contents, see his earlier journal article Brachtendorf (1998, esp. 42–45). Also helpful are the reviews of this work by R.A. Markus (2001) and Roland Teske (2002). I would also like to thank Jos. Lam Cong Quy OSA of the Augustinus-Institut, Würzburg, for his helpful comments on Brachtendorf's work.

[43] Still, it is an achievement prefigured in the work of Biolo (1979).

[44] The material on realms of meaning is contained in Lonergan (1972, 81–85). I have tried to give my own expression of these realms where possible.

[45] Lonergan position, as quoted by Matthew L. Lamb (1981, 293), is as follows: "The argument is: that the prior is not object as object or subject as object; there only remains subject as subject, and this subject as subject is both reality and discoverable through consciousness. The argument does not prove that in the subject as subject we shall find the evidence, norms, invariants and principles for a critique of horizons; it proves that unless we find it there, we shall not find it at all."

[46] It is perhaps this aspect which places us at such a distance from what he is doing, as Christian common sense struggles to incorporate the results of critical historical readings of Scripture. My own students' reaction to Augustinian exegesis here was to find it laboured to the point of perplexity on their part. His fundamental commitment to the truth of the scriptural word was not part of their intellectual horizon.

[47] The translation by Hill has a flash "from the corner of your eye" which is not in the Latin, and in the context misses the point.

[48] A different solution to this problem might be to note that the appetite Augustine identifies is pure potency, and hence does not form a suitable analogue for the pure act of divinity. See Stevenson (2000).

[49] Modern translations become almost useless in this context. Translators are simply not familiar enough with the issues of consciousness to know how best to translate the original text. The article by Biolo (1979) represents a good example of someone who is aware of the basic issues facing a translator of Augustine in this regard.

[50] The conclusion of Book 10 seems to introduce the triad of memory, understanding and will without any real explanation. Certainly it puzzles Merriell (1990, 27) and it has puzzled me. The solution has been offered by Biolo (1979) where he argues that *memoria sui* is a technical term in Augustine for the primitive self-presence of the subject.

[51] While Hill at least notes that something different is happening in Books 12–15, the works of Cavadini and Brachtendorf provide no explanation for this resurgence in use of the Scriptures.

[52] If the phrase "image of God" is the recurrent theme of Book 12, the word "seek," as in "seek his face," "seek the Lord," "seek Him" etc, is the recurrent theme of Book 15.

[53] Various computer searches of standard databases, CPLI and ATLA Religions database, as well as of Lonergan Studies Newsletter produced very little by way of comparative studies or even connections between Augustine and Lonergan, apart from the work of Biolo and a chapter in a book by Richard M. Liddy (1993, 50–73).

[54] I argue this position more fully elsewhere (Ormerod 2000, esp. chap. 7). See the chapter following on the psychological analogy.

[55] This chapter is a revised version of an earlier journal article by Ormerod (2001).

[56] Here I shall draw on the article by Hunt (1998). Hunt has synthesized a number of Balthasar's writings (1970; 1983; 1993).

[57] Doran refers to the "scattered references" to Scotus to be found in Hans Urs von Balthasar's work (1991, 585-86 n.46).

[58] For an excellent exposition of "intelligible emanation" see Frederick E. Crowe (2000).

[59] See for example the encyclical, *Veritatis Splendour.*

[60] A further instance of such a capitulation is the withdrawal from "natural theology" among theologians, under the unquestioned assumption that it is "not possible to prove the existence of God." This position concedes too much to those who wish to keep religion in the private sphere. In this regard it is interesting to note that Lonergan viewed the psychological analogy as "a prolongation of natural theology" (1997, 215).

[61] For a detailed examination of Thomas' theory of appropriations, see, Timothy L. Smith (1999).

[62] I acknowledge the assistance of Paul Oxley and his unpublished thesis (2003) in this section and the section below on Denis Edwards.

[63] See Lonergan (1972, 76–81). For its Trinitarian application see Kelly (1989, 18–19).

[64] See Mansini (2000) for a detailed criticism of Balthasar from the perspective of the Western tradition, on the question of divine immutability. One senses Mansini's frustration with Balthasar when he concludes that: "To say that revelation, as read by Balthasar, trumps Aristotle here is not to preserve revelation and therefore the autonomy of theology; it is to say that grace does not complete but rather destroys nature, that faith kills and does not perfect reason" (2000, 519).

[65] See the work of Anne Hunt (1997) for accounts of Balthasar, Ghislain Lafont, François Durwell and Sebastian Moore.

[66] This suggestion is meant to complement the conclusion drawn by Hunt, namely, that Balthasar operates from an aesthetically differentiated consciousness (1997, 152).

[67] Such a position is present in Augustine inasmuch as he did not successfully distinguish between the natural and supernatural orders. Edwards' inspiration (1995, 101–110) is more the theology of Bonaventure. Another modern exponent of this trend to supernaturalise the natural is the radical orthodoxy of John Milbank (1991, passim).

[68] See, for example, White's thesis (1995) that Christianity is in fact responsible for our current ecological crisis. It has been subject to

criticism from a number of sources: Collins (1995, 87–123); Alister McGrath (2003, esp. xv–xvii). McGrath even states that White's thesis is "why I decided to write this book" (2003, xvii).

[69] This chapter is a revised version of an earlier journal article by Ormerod (2003c).

[70] This same suggestion has been made by John M. McDermott (1986, 87–123, 297–327). McDermott comes to his evaluation (ibid. 308–325) after a long and detailed exposition of Rahner's work. I think the blurring is clearly evident already in Rahner's Trinitarian material.

[71] While I share many of Molnar's concerns as to Coffey's conclusions, I do not accept his Barthian presuppositions, particularly a rejection of any role for natural theology in Trinitarian theology. Coffey (2002) has completely rejected Molnar's criticisms.

[72] See also Keaty (2000) for a thorough analysis of Aquinas on this point; and Congar (1983, 1:85–90) for the weaknesses of the "mutual love" analogy.

[73] While the subordinationist position is rare these days, the tendency to tritheism is relatively strong. I have already noted this in relation to the work of Moltmann and Volf.

[74] Doran suggests that Rahner's "system" falls into this problem leading to the eventual denial of the immanent Trinity. Here I suggest it also leads to a denial of the *filioque*.

[75] The document Coffey is responding to is entitled, "The Greek and Latin Traditions Regarding the Procession of the Holy Spirit," published in *L'Osservatore Romano* 20 Sept, 1995, 3, 6, at 3.

[76] It should be stated that while Coffey (1999a, 16–17) appeals to Lonergan's three-fold structure of experience-understanding-judgment to justify his own approach his application of this bears no resemblance to Lonergan's own theological method as spelt out in *Method in Theology*.

[77] One may ask where the *filioque* sits in this analysis. For Augustine the *filioque* is a conclusion from Scripture and the dogmatic facts of the processions, based on their logical clarification through notions of persons and relations. By the time of Aquinas, it was considered a dogmatic fact, which may be rendered analogously intelligible through the psychological analogy.

[78] For an analysis and critique of Schillebeeckx, see Ormerod (1993).

[79] A good account of the trajectory of Hick's theology, on which I have drawn here, can be found in Gavin D'Costa's *The Meeting of Religions and the Trinity, Faith Meets Faith* (2000, 24–30).

[80] This translation is made by Robert Doran from Bernard J. F. Lonergan's *De Deo Trino, Pars Systematica* (1964, 234–35).

[81] See his soon to be published work, *What is Systematic Theology?*

Bibliography

Augustine. 1963. *The Trinity*. Trans. Stephen McKenna. *Fathers of the Church*. Washington, DC: Catholic University of America Press.

———. *The Trinity*. 1991. Translated by Edmund Hill. Edited by John E. Rotelle O.S.A. Brooklyn, NY: New City Press.

Ayres, Lewis. 1998. "The Christological Context of Augustine's *De Trinitate* XIII: Toward Relocating Books VIII–XV." *Augustinian Studies* 29: 111–39.

Balthasar, Hans Urs von. 1970. *Love Alone: The Way of Revelation*. London: Sheed and Ward.

———. 1983. *Seeing the Form*. Translated by Erasmo Leiva-Merikakis. Vol. 1, *The Glory of the Lord: A Theological Aesthetics*. San Francisco/New York: Ignatius Press/Crossroad Publications.

———. 1991. *The Realm of Metaphysics in the Modern World*. Translated by Erasmo Leiva-Merikakis. Vol. 5, *The Glory of the Lord*. San Francisco/New York: Ignatius Press/Crossroad Publications.

———. 1993. *Mysterium Paschale: The Mystery of Easter*. Grand Rapids, MI: W.B. Eerdmans.

Barnes, Michel René. 1995. "The Use of Augustine in Contemporary Trinitarian Theology." *Theological Studies* 56: 237–50.

———. 1999. "Rereading Augustine's Theology of the Trinity." In *The Trinity: An Interdisciplinary Symposium on the Trinity*. S. Davis, D. Kendall and G. O'Collins. New York: Oxford University Press: 145–176.

Barron, Robert. 2000. "Beyond Beige Catholicism." *Church* 16, Summer: 5–10.

Barth, Karl. 1936. *Church Dogmatics*. Translated by G.T. Thomson. Edited by Geoffrey William Bromiley and Thomas Forsyth Torrance. Edinburgh: T. & T. Clark.

Bettenson, Henry. 1970. *The Later Christian Fathers; a Selection from the Writings of the Fathers from St. Cyril of Jerusalem to St. Leo the Great*. London/New York: Oxford University Press.

Biolo, Salvino. 1969. *La Coscienza Nel De Trinitate Di S. Agostino*. Rome: Analecta Gregoriana.

————. 1979. "A Lonerganian Approach to St Augustine's Interpretation of Consciousness." *Science et Esprit* 31: 323–41.

Boff, Leonardo. 1978. *Jesus Christ Liberator: A Critical Christology for Our Time.* Maryknoll, NY: Orbis Books.

————. 1988. *Trinity and Society, Theology and Liberation Series.* Maryknoll, NY: Orbis Books.

Brachtendorf, Johannes. 1998. "' … *Prius Esse Cogitare Quam Credere*' a Natural Understanding of 'Trinity' in St Augustine?" *Augustinian Studies* 29: 35–45.

————. 2000. *Die Struktur Des Menschlichen Geistes Nach Augustinus: Selbstreflexion Und Erkenntis Gottes in "De Trinitate," Paradeigmata Series 19.* Hamburg: Meiner.

Bracken, Joseph. 1992. Review of *God for us: the Trinity and Christian Life* by Catherine LaCugna. *Theological Studies* 53:558-60.

Brown, Peter. 1967. *Augustine of Hippo.* Berkeley: University of California Press.

Burrell, David B. 1979. *Aquinas: God and Action.* Notre Dame, Ind.: University of Notre Dame Press.

Cavadini, John C. 1992. "The Structure and Intention of Augustine's *De Trinitate.*" *Augustinian Studies* 23: 103–23.

————. 1997. "The Quest for Truth in Augustine's *De Trinitate.*" *Theological Studies* 58: 429–40.

Coakley, Sarah. 1999. "'Persons' in the 'Social' Doctrine of the Trinity: A Critique of Current Analytic Discussion." In *The Trinity: An Interdisciplinary Symposium on the Trinity.* S. Davis, D. Kendall and G. O'Collins. New York: Oxford University Press: 123–144.

Coffey, David. 1979. *Grace: The Gift of the Holy Spirit.* Sydney: Catholic Institute of Sydney.

————. 1984. "The 'Incarnation' of the Holy Spirit in Christ." *Theological Studies* 45: 466–80.

————. 1986. "A Proper Mission of the Holy Spirit." *Theological Studies* 47: 227–50.

————. 1999a. *Deus Trinitas: The Doctrine of the Triune God.* New York: Oxford University Press.

————. 1999b "The Theandric Nature of Christ." *Theological Studies* 60: 405–31.

―――. 2002. "In Response to Paul Molnar." *Irish Theological Quarterly* 67: 375–78.

―――. 2003. "The Roman 'Clarification' of the Doctrine of the *Filioque.*" *International Journal of Systematic Theology* 5: 3–15.

Collins, Paul. 1995. *God's Earth: Religion as If Matter Really Mattered.* Melbourne: Dove.

Congar, Yves. 1983. *I Believe in the Holy Spirit.* Translated by David Smith. 3 vols. New York/London: Seabury Press/G. Chapman.

Crowe, Frederick E. 1992. *Lonergan, Outstanding Christian Thinkers.* Collegeville, MN: Liturgical Press.

―――. 2000. "For Inserting a New Question (26a) in the Prima Pars." *Thomist* 64: 565–80.

Dallavalle, Nancy. 1998. "Revisiting Rahner: On the Theological Status of Trinitarian Theology." *Irish Theological Quarterly* 63: 133–50.

D'Costa, Gavin. 2000. *The Meeting of Religions and the Trinity, Faith Meets Faith.* Maryknoll, NY: Orbis Books.

―――. 2000. *Sexing the Trinity: Gender, Culture and the Divine.* London: SCM Press.

Dewart, Leslie. 1966. *The Future of Belief; Theism in a World Come of Age.* New York: Herder and Herder.

―――. 1969. *The Foundations of Belief.* New York: Herder and Herder.

DiNoia, Joseph. 1993. Review of *God for us: the Trinity and Christian Life*, by Catherine LaCugna. *Modern Theology* 9 (April): 214-16.

Doran, Robert M. 1990. *Theology and the Dialectics of History.* Toronto: University of Toronto Press.

―――. 1997. "Lonergan and Balthasar : Methodological Considerations." *Theological Studies.* 58: 61–84.

―――. 1998. "Bernard Lonergan and the Functions of Systematic Theology." *Theological Studies* 59: 569–607.

―――. 2000. "The First Chapter of *De Deo Trino, Pars Systematica*: The Issues." *Method: Journal of Lonergan Studies* 18: 27–48.

―――. 2001. "*Intelligentia Fidei* in *De Deo Trino, Pars Systematica.*" *Method: Journal of Lonergan Studies* 19: 35–83.

Douglass, Bruce, and Hollenbach David. 1994. *Catholicism and Liberalism: Contributions to American Public Philosophy.* Cambridge: Cambridge University Press.

Dupuis, Jacques. 1997. *Toward a Christian Theology of Religious Pluralism.* Maryknoll, NY: Orbis Books.

Edwards, Denis. 1995. *Jesus the Wisdom of God: An Ecological Theology.* Maryknoll, NY: Orbis Books.

———. 1999. *The God of Evolution: A Trinitarian Theology.* New York: Paulist Press.

Fatula, Mary Ann. 1990. *The Triune God of Christian Faith.* Collegeville, MN: Liturgical Press.

Fox, Patricia. 2001. *God as Communion: John Zizioulas, Elizabeth Johnson, and the Retrieval of the Symbol of the Triune God.* Collegeville, MN: Liturgical Press.

Gunton, Colin E. 1990. "Augustine, the Trinity and the Theological Crisis of the West." *Scottish Journal of Theology* 43: 33–58.

———. 1993. *The One, the Three, and the Many: God, Creation, and the Culture of Modernity.* Cambridge/New York: Cambridge University Press.

———. 1997. *The Promise of Trinitarian Theology.* 2nd ed. Edinburgh: T&T Clark.

Haight, Roger. 1992. "The Case for Spirit Christology." *Theological Studies* 53: 257–87.

———. 1999. *Jesus, Symbol of God.* Maryknoll, NY: Orbis Books.

Helminiak, Daniel A. 1986. *The Same Jesus: A Contemporary Christology.* Chicago: Loyola University Press.

Hick, John. 1974. *God and the Universe of Faiths; Essays in the Philosophy of Religion.* New York: St. Martin's Press.

———. 1985. *Problems of Religious Pluralism.* New York: St. Martin's Press.

———. 1993. *The Metaphor of God Incarnate: Christology in a Pluralistic Age.* Louisville, KY: Westminster/John Knox Press.

———. 1995. *A Christian Theology of Religions: The Rainbow of Faiths.* Louisville, KY: Westminster John Knox Press.

Hill, Edmund. 1985. *The Mystery of the Trinity.* London: Geoffrey Chapman.

Hill, William J. 1982. *The Three-Personed God: The Trinity as a Mystery of Salvation.* Washington, DC: Catholic University of America Press.

Hunt, Anne. 1997. *The Trinity and the Paschal Mystery: A Development in Recent Catholic Theology*. Collegeville, MN: Liturgical Press.

———. 1998. "Psychological Analogy and Paschal Mystery in Trinitarian Theology." *Theological Studies* 59: 197–218.

Johnson, Elizabeth A. 1992. *She Who Is: The Mystery of God in Feminist Theological Discourse*. New York: Crossroad.

Kasper, Walter. 1984. *The God of Jesus Christ*. Translated by Matthew J. O'Connell. New York: Crossroad.

———. 1989. *Theology and Church*. Translated by Margaret Kohl. New York: Crossroad.

Keaty, Anthony. 2000. "The Holy Spirit Proceeding as Mutual Love: An Interpretation of Aquinas' *Summa Theologiae*, I.37." *Angelicum* 77: 533–57.

Kelly, Anthony. 1989. *The Trinity of Love: A Theology of the Christian God*. Wilmington, DE: Michael Glazier.

———. 1996. "The 'Horrible Wrappers' of Aquinas' God." *Pacifica* 9: 185–203.

Kuhn, Thomas S. 1996. *The Structure of Scientific Revolutions*. 3rd ed. Chicago: University of Chicago Press.

LaCugna, Catherine Mowry. 1993. *God for Us: The Trinity and Christian Life*. San Francisco: HarperSanFrancisco.

Lamb, Matthew L. 1981. "Methodology, Metascience and Political Theology." In *Lonergan Workshop Vol.2*, edited by Frederick G. Lawrence, 281–403. Lanham, MD: Scholars Press.

Liddy, Richard M. 1993. *Transforming Light: Intellectual Conversion in the Early Lonergan*. Collegeville, MN.: Liturgical Press.

Lindbeck, George A. 1984. *The Nature of Doctrine: Religion and Theology in a Postliberal Age*. Philadelphia: Westminster Press.

Lonergan, Bernard J. F. 1958. *Insight: A Study of Human Understanding*. London: DLT.

———. 1964. *De Deo Trino, Pars Systematica*. Rome: Gregorian University Press.

———. 1972. *Method in Theology*. London: DLT.

———. 1976. *The Way to Nicea: The Dialectical Development of Trinitarian Theology*. Translated by Conn O'Donovan. London: DLT.

———. 1985. "Christology Today: Methodological Reflections." In *A Third Collection*, edited by F. Crowe, 74–99. New York: Paulist.

————. 1992. *Insight: A Study of Human Understanding.* Edited by Crowe Frederick E. and Robert M. Doran. Vol. 3, *Collected Works of Bernard Lonergan.* Toronto: University of Toronto Press.

————, 1997. *Verbum: Word and Idea in Aquinas.* Edited by Frederick E. Crowe and Robert M. Doran. Vol. 2, *Collected Works of Bernard Lonergan.* Toronto: University of Toronto Press.

————. 2002. *The Ontological and Psychological Constitution of Christ.* Translated by Michael G. Shields. Edited by Frederick E. Crowe and Robert M. Doran. Vol. 7, *Collected Works of Bernard Lonergan.* Toronto: University of Toronto Press.

Lossky, Vladimir. 1978. *Orthodox Theology: An Introduction.* Translated by Ian and Ihita Kesarcodi-Watson. Crestwood, NY: St Vladimir's Seminary Press.

MacIntyre, Alasdair. 1984. *After Virtue: A Study in Moral Theory.* 2nd ed. Notre Dame, IN: University of Notre Dame Press.

————. 1988. *Whose Justice? Which Rationality?* Notre Dame, IN: University of Notre Dame Press.

————. 1990. *Three Rival Versions of Moral Enquiry: Encyclopaedia, Genealogy, and Tradition.* Notre Dame, IN: University of Notre Dame Press.

Mansini, Guy. 1988. "Quasi-Formal Causality and Change in the Other: A Note on Karl Rahner's Christology." *Thomist* 52: 293–306.

————. 2000. "Balthasar and the Theodramatic Enrichment of the Trinity." *Thomist* 64: 499–519.

Margerie, Bertrand de. 1982. *The Christian Trinity in History.* Still River, MA: St. Bede's Publications.

McDermott, John M. 1986. "The Christologies of Karl Rahner." *Gregorianum* 67: 87–123; 297–327.

McGrath, Alister. 2003. *The Re-Enchantment of Nature: Science, Religion, and the Human Sense of Wonder.* London: Hodder & Stoughton.

Markus, R.A. 2001. Review of *Die Structur des menschlichen Geistes nach Augustinus: Selbstreflexion und Erkenntnis Gottes in "De trinitate"*, by Johannes Brachtendorf. *Augustinian Studies* 32:151-53.

Merriell, D. Juvenal. 1990. *To the Image of the Trinity: A Study in the Development of Aquinas' Teaching.* Toronto: Pontifical Institute of Mediaeval Studies.

Metz, Johannes Baptist. 1980. *Faith in History and Society: Toward a Practical Fundamental Theology*. Translated by David Smith. New York: Seabury Press.

Milbank, John. 1991. *Theology and Social Theory: Beyond Secular Reason*. Cambridge, MA: B. Blackwell.

———. 1997. *The Word Made Strange: Theology, Language, Culture*. Cambridge, MA: Blackwell Publishers.

Molnar, Paul D. 1985. "Can We Know God Directly? Rahner's Solution from Experience." *Theological Studies* 46: 228–61.

———. 2002. "*Deus Trinitas*: Some Dogmatic Implications of David Coffey's Biblical Approach to the Trinity." *Irish Theological Quarterly* 67: 33–54.

Moloney, Raymond. 1999. *The Knowledge of Christ*. London/New York: Continuum.

Moltmann, Jürgen. 1981. *The Trinity and the Kingdom of God: The Doctrine of God*. London: SCM Press.

O'Collins, Gerald. 1999. *The Tripersonal God: Understanding and Interpreting the Trinity*. New York: Paulist Press.

O'Donnell, John J. 1988. *The Mystery of the Triune God*. London: Sheed & Ward.

Ogilvie, Matthew. 2001. *Faith Seeking Understanding: The Functional Specialty, Systematics, in Bernard Lonergan's Method in Theology*. Milwaukee, WI: Marquette University Press.

Ormerod, Neil. 1993a. "Schillebeeckx's Philosophic Prolegomenon: A Dialectic Analysis." In *Australian Lonergan Workshop*, edited by William Danaher, 69–78. Lanham, MD: University Press of America.

———. 1993b. "The Transcultural Significance of the Council of Chalcedon." *Australasian Catholic Record* LXX: 322–32.

———. 1999. "'It Is Easy to See': The Footnotes of John Milbank." *Philosophy and Theology* 11 (2): 257–64.

———. 2000. *Method, Meaning and Revelation: The Meaning and Function of Revelation in Bernard Lonergan's Method in Theology*. Lanham, MD: University Press of America.

———. 2001. "The Psychological Analogy for the Trinity—at Odds with Modernity." *Pacifica* 14: 281–94.

————. 2003a. "Augustine and the Trinity—Whose Crisis?" *Pacifica* 16: 17–32.

————. 2003b. "Augustine's *De Trinitate* and Lonergan's Realms of Meaning." *Theological Studies* 64: 773–94.

————. 2003c. "Wrestling with Rahner on the Trinity." *Irish Theological Quarterly* 68: 213–27.

Oxley, Paul. 2003. "Trinity, Ecology and Cosmology: The Works of Denis Edwards and Tony Kelly." MTh(Hons), Sydney College of Divinity.

Pannenberg, Wolfhart. 1991. *Systematic Theology.* Translated by Geoffrey W. Bromiley. 3 vols. Grand Rapids, MI: Eerdmans.

Pelikan, Jaroslav Jan. 1971. *The Emergence of the Catholic Tradition (100–600).* Chicago: University of Chicago Press.

Rahner, Karl. 1974. *The Trinity.* New York: Seabury Press.

————. 1982. *Foundations of Christian Faith: An Introduction to the Idea of Christianity.* New York: Crossroad.

Ratzinger, Joseph. 1988. "Foundations and Approaches of Biblical Exegesis." *Origins* 17/35: 593, 595–602.

Schillebeeckx, Edward. 1980. *Christ, the Christian Experience in the Modern World.* London: SCM Press.

————. 1990. *Church: The Human Story of God.* Translated by John Bowden. New York: Crossroad.

Schleiermacher, Friedrich. 1928. *The Christian Faith.* Edited by H. R. Mackintosh and James Stuart Stewart. Edinburgh: T. & T. Clark.

Siri, Cardinal. 1975. *Gethsemane: Reflexions Sur Le Mouvement Theologique Contemporain.* Rome: Editions de la Fraternite de la Tres Sainte Vierge Marie.

Smith, Timothy L. 1999. "The Context and Character of Thomas's Theory of Appropriations." *Thomist* 63: 579–612.

Stevenson, William. 2000. "The Problem of Trinitarian Processions in Thomas's Roman Commentary." *Thomist* 64: 619–29.

Studer, Basil. 1997. "History and Faith in Augustine's *De Trinitate*." *Augustinian Studies* 28: 7–50.

Teske, Roland. 2002. Review of *Die Structur des menschlichen Geistes nach Augustinus: Selbstreflexion und Erkenntnis Gottes in "De trinitate"*, by Johannes Brachtendorf. *Journal of Early Christian Studies* 10: 414-16.

Torrance, Thomas Forsyth. 1996. *The Christian Doctrine of God, One Being Three Persons.* Edinburgh: T. &T. Clark.

Volf, Miroslav. 1998. *After Our Likeness: The Church as the Image of the Trinity.* Grand Rapids, MI: William B. Eerdmans.

Vorgrimler, Herbert. 1986. *Understanding Karl Rahner: An Introduction to His Life and Thought.* New York: Crossroad.

Weinandy, Thomas G. 1995. *The Father's Spirit of Sonship: Reconceiving the Trinity.* Edinburgh: T & T Clark.

———. 1999. *Does God Suffer?* Notre Dame, IN: University of Notre Dame.

White, Lynn. 1995. "The Historical Roots of Our Ecological Crisis." In *Readings in Ecology and Feminist Theology,* edited by Mary McKinnon and Moni McIntyre, 25–35. Kansas City: Sheed & Ward.

Zizioulas, John. 1985. *Being as Communion: Studies in Personhood and the Church.* Crestwood, NY: St. Vladimir's Seminary Press.

———. 1994. "The Church as Communion." *St Vladimir's Theological Quarterly* 38: 3–16.

Index

DATE DUE

#47-0108 Peel Off Pressure Sensitive